THE COMPLETE

NINJA FOODI XL PRO

AIR FRYER OVEN

COOKBOOK

1000-DAY QUICK, EASY, TENDER AND CRISPY NINJA FOODI RECIPES TO LIVE HEALTHIER AND HAPPIER

MARK THORNBURG

CONTENTS

INTRODUCTION

How Does the Ninja Foodi XL Pro Air Fryer Oven Work?

An air fryer oven takes the latest craze of air fryers that use convection heat to cook rapidly in a confined space and combines it in a toaster oven with other cooking functions, like baking, broiling, toasting and sometimes rotisserie-cooking and dehydrating too. It is basically a multi-function countertop convection oven with a motorized fan on top of the unit that blows the hot air down directly on foods, rather than circulating the air around the oven cavity. It's perfect for the cook who would like to have the ability to air fry, but wants to have multiple cooking functions without sacrificing more counter space.

The Benefits of Owning the Ninja Foodi XL Pro Air Fryer Oven

1. Takes Up Less Space

You don't have to worry about where to put your air fryer oven because it doesn't require much space. It is smaller compared to the convection oven. You only need around 1 foot cubed space for this kitchen device. When you are done with your air fryer oven, you can safely keep it away and bring it out the next time you want to use it. Majority of people keep their air fryer ovens on the kitchen countertops. This is something you can do if you're going to enjoy the pleasing sight of your air fryer oven.

2. Safe to Use

The process of deep frying foods has some dangers attached to it. Imagine throwing in French fries in extremely hot oil. Accidents can occur. For example, the splattering oil could burn you. Also, you can cause a fire that can destroy property or even worse, lead to death.

You don't have to worry about these unpleasant occurrences when using an air fryer because all the cooking happens inside it. The appliance is locked, and there's no splattering oil.

You can't be exposed to radiation when using air fryer like you would when using a microwave.

It gets better with air fryers. These kitchen appliances have auto shutdown. This means that the fryer turns itself off after your food is ready. Therefore, you won't have burnt food.

3.   Preserves Nutrients

The process of air frying food protects the food from losing too much moisture. The fact that this method uses little oil and there's circulation of hot air creates a coating on the food. Therefore, your food will keep most of its nutrients.

If you are preparing your food with the aim of enjoying the nutrients, then an air fryer will help you to do that.

4.   No Oil Smell

Most people don't like to smell like food. Imagine making delicious French fries at home and then smelling like them as you move around interacting with people.

Your entire home could also be smelling of French fries from the oil used to prepare it. This can happen if you use the normal deep fat fryer. The oil can even splatter around the kitchen increasing the concentration of the cooking smells.

The air fryer oven ensures you don't have any smells since all the oil and smells are enclosed within the appliance.

5.   Cooks with Almost No Oil

We know how dangerous too much oil can be to our bodies. The air fryer oven saves us from complications arising from taking in a lot of oil. When using air fryer oven, you'll only use about 20% of the oil you normally use to cook.

There are some models that do not use any oil at all. This means that you'll take in less fat and calories which is good news if you're trying to lose weight or stay healthy. Also, you'll spend less money on cooking oil.

6.   Makes Low Fat Food with Fewer Calories

If you want to take in fewer calories and fat, buy an air fryer oven. With this cooking appliance, you'll use about one tablespoon of oil or less to prepare your food.

You'll food tasty and crunchy food without adding any calories to your body. That's the perfect situation. When you deep fry foods, the food takes in a lot of oil because it has been dipped into the oil. The fact that this doesn't happen with an air fryer oven makes it possible to enjoy food with less fat and calories.

Useful Tips Before Using Your Ninja Foodi XL Pro Air Fryer Tips

1. Make sure that the voltage indicated on the appliance corresponds to the local available voltage before you connect the appliance.

2. Do not use the appliance if the plug or the power cord or the appliance itself is damaged.

3. Never immerse the cord, plug, or housing, which contains electrical components and heating elements, in water or any other liquid, nor rinse under tap water. See instructions for cleaning.

4. Do not let any water or other liquid enter the appliance to prevent electric shock.

5. Always put the ingredients to be fried in the accessories included to prevent them from coming into contact with the heating elements.

6. Do not cover the air inlet and the air outlet while the appliance is operating.

7. Do not add oil to the drip tray or pans, as this may cause a fire hazard.

8. While cooking, the internal temperature of the unit reaches several hundred degrees Fahrenheit. To avoid personal injury, never place hands inside the unit unless it is thoroughly cooled.

9. Keep the power cord away from hot surfaces.

10. Do not place the appliance on or near combustible materials such as a tablecloth or curtain.

11. Use only on a level, dry, and heat-resistant surface.

12. Do not place the appliance against a wall or against other appliances. Leave at least 3.9 in. (10 cm) free space on the back, sides, and above the appliance. Do not place anything on top of the appliance.

13. Do not use the appliance for any other purpose than described in this manual.

14. WARNING: During hot air frying, hot steam is released through the air outlet openings on the back of the air fryer oven. Keep your hands and face at a safe distance from the steam and from the air outlet openings. Also be careful of hot steam and air when you open the door of the appliance.

Tips on How to Clean Built on Grease of the Ninja Foodi XL Pro Air Fryer Oven

Of course even with wiping it down after every use (or you forget to wipe it down), you will inevitably get built on grease. The following is 2 Part Step to cleaning built on grease.

Cleaning Part 1: Baking Soda Paste

The first part of the deep cleaning process starts with making and applying a baking soda paste.

➢ Mix 1/4 cup Baking Soda with 2 Tbl Warm Water.
➢ Mix 1/2 cup Baking Soda with Warm Water.

Using a Paint brush or toothbrush, apply the paste to the sides, back, and ceiling of the oven. In the pictures below I only applied it to half in order to do a side by side comparison. However, you will apply the paste to the inside of the entire oven.

Things to remember when applying the paste:

1. Constantly mix the paste while applying it. The baking soda tends to separate from the water.
2. Remove the trays and the drip tray.
3. You can place a piece of parchment paper or a paper towel on the floor of the oven to help with clean up.
4. When applying the paste to the ceiling of the oven, don't apply it to any place you can't reach with a sponge to clean it off.
5. As the paste dries, it will turn bright white. You can see where you missed applying the paste and add more if needed.

Once you have applied the paste to the inside of the oven, the most important part is——

Let it sit for 12 to 24 hours!

This is the most important part. Baking soda is a basic solution and works great to cut through acidic grease. However, it is not very strong, so it needs time to work.

When you are ready to remove the paste you will need:

➢ Large bowl of water
➢ Sponge with a non-scratch scouring side (or you can use a heavy duty brillo sponge that has been used and is worn down)
➢ toothbrush
➢ straw cleaning brush

➢ Norwex cloth

As you use the sponge to remove the baking soda, constantly rinse it int he bowl of water and wring it out. Use the toothbrush and straw brush to get into the tight spaces.

Do NOT press hard while scrubbing. Just take your time. This is a slow process but worth it!

Once you have removed the baking soda, use the Norwex cloth to wipe down the sides, making sure to get off any residue that is left.

You can stop at this point, but if you are like me and want your oven to look as close to brand new as possible, then the next step is….

Cleaning Part 2: Steam Cleaning

The baking soda does a great job cutting through the first few layers of the baked on grease. To get the rest off, the best thing I have found to use is my steam cleaner. The one I recommend is the Dupray Multipurpose Steam Cleaner.

Of course I don't just use this steam cleaner for my oven. It's one of my favorite things and I use it to clean just about everything.

Use the brush end of your steam cleaner to clean the sides. The trick is to steam the grease for about 10 seconds in order to allow the hot steam to melt the grease. Then you can wipe it away.

Use the fine nozzle to get into the tight spaces like at the top edge of the Vortex Plus and the metal brackets on the Omni/Omni Plus.

The steam cleaner is also fabulous at getting in the hard to reach space where the door clips in on the Vortex Plus as well as the edge between the door and the glass on the Omni/Omni Plus.

Do NOT use the steam on the heating elements, heating coil, rotisserie knob, or on the ceiling near the fan.

BREAKFAST

Hot Italian-style Sub

Servings:3

Cooking Time: 15 Minutes

Ingredients:

- ➢ 3 Italian-style hoagie rolls
- ➢ 3 tablespoons unsalted butter, softened
- ➢ 1 teaspoon Italian seasoning
- ➢ ½ teaspoon garlic powder
- ➢ 9 slices salami
- ➢ 12 slices pepperoni
- ➢ 3 thin slices ham
- ➢ 3 tablespoons giardiniera mix, chopped
- ➢ 6 tablespoons shredded mozzarella cheese

Directions:

1. Preheat the toaster oven to 350°F. Split the rolls lengthwise, cutting almost but not quite though the roll. Place the sandwiches in a 12 x 12-inch baking pan, side by side with the open side face up.

2. Combine the butter, Italian seasoning, and garlic powder in a small bowl. Spread evenly on the inside of the hoagie rolls.

3. Layer a third of the salami, pepperoni, and ham on each sandwich. Sprinkle with the giardiniera mix and mozzarella cheese.

4. Bake for 10 to 15 minutes or until heated through and the cheese is melted.

Apple Maple Pudding

Servings: 4

Cooking Time: 20 Minutes

Ingredients:

- ➢ Pudding mixture:
- ➢ 2 eggs
- ➢ ½ cup brown sugar
- ➢ 4 tablespoons maple syrup
- ➢ 3 tablespoons unbleached flour
- ➢ 1 teaspoon baking powder
- ➢ 1 teaspoon vanilla extract
- ➢ ¼ cup chopped raisins
- ➢ ¼ cup chopped walnuts
- ➢ 2 medium apples, peeled and chopped

Directions:

1. Preheat the toaster oven to 350° F.
2. Combine the pudding mixture ingredients in a medium bowl, beating the eggs, sugar, and maple syrup together first, then adding the flour, baking powder, and vanilla. Add the raisins, nuts, and apples and mix thoroughly. Pour into an oiled or nonstick 8½ × 8½ × 2-inch square baking (cake) pan.
3. BAKE for 20 minutes, or until a toothpick inserted in the center comes out clean.
4. BROIL for 5 minutes, or until the top is lightly browned.

Homemade Biscuits

Servings: 12

Cooking Time: 28 Minutes

Ingredients:

- 1 1/2 cups milk
- 1 tablespoon white vinegar
- 4 cups all-purpose flour
- 1/4 cup sugar
- 1 tablespoon plus 1 1/2 teaspoons baking powder
- 1 teaspoon salt
- 1 cup unsalted butter, cut into pieces
- Sausage Gravy

Directions:

1. Preheat the toaster oven to 375°F. Line a cookie sheet with parchment paper.
2. In a small bowl, stir milk and vinegar until blended. Set aside.
3. In a large bowl, combine flour, sugar, baking powder and salt. Cut in butter with a fork or a pastry blender until coarse crumbs form. Stir in the milk mixture until moistened (dough will be slightly moist).
4. On a well floured surface, roll dough to 3/4-inch thickness. Cut with a 3-inch round cookie cutter and arrange 2-inches apart on cookie sheet. Repeat with remaining dough.
5. Bake 26 to 28 minutes or until lightly browned.
6. Serve with Sausage Gravy, if desired.

Pecan-topped Baked Oatmeal

Servings: 6

Cooking Time: 45 Minutes

Ingredients:

- ➢ 2 tablespoons unsalted butter, plus additional for the pan
- ➢ 2 large eggs
- ➢ 3 cups whole milk
- ➢ ¼ cup packed dark brown sugar
- ➢ 1 teaspoon ground cinnamon
- ➢ 1 teaspoon pure vanilla extract
- ➢ ¼ teaspoon kosher salt
- ➢ 3 cups old-fashioned oats
- ➢ TOPPING
- ➢ ¼ cup packed dark brown sugar
- ➢ ½ cup chopped pecans
- ➢ Fresh blueberries (optional)
- ➢ Milk (optional)

Directions:

1. Lightly butter an 8 x 8-inch square baking pan.
2. Melt 2 tablespoons butter; set aside to cool slightly.
3. Whisk the eggs in a large bowl. Add the milk, brown sugar, cinnamon, vanilla, and salt and whisk to combine. Stir in the oats. Stir in the melted butter. Pour into the prepared pan. Cover and refrigerate overnight.
4. When ready to bake, preheat the toaster oven to 350°F. Gently stir the oat mixture in the baking pan.
5. Make the topping: Blend the brown sugar and pecans in a small bowl. Sprinkle the pecan mixture over the top of the oats. Bake, uncovered, for 40 to 45 minutes or until it is set and a knife inserted in the center comes out clean.
6. Sprinkle with fresh blueberries, if desired. Spoon into bowls and serve with milk to drizzle on top.

Cheddar Cheese Biscuits

Servings: 8   Cooking Time: 22 Minutes

Ingredients:

- 2⅓ cups self-rising flour
- 2 tablespoons sugar
- ½ cup butter (1 stick), frozen for 15 minutes
- ½ cup grated Cheddar cheese, plus more to melt on top
- 1⅓ cups buttermilk
- 1 cup all-purpose flour, for shaping
- 1 tablespoon butter, melted

Directions:

1. Line a buttered 7-inch metal cake pan with parchment paper or a silicone liner.

2. Combine the flour and sugar in a large mixing bowl. Grate the butter into the flour. Add the grated cheese and stir to coat the cheese and butter with flour. Then add the buttermilk and stir just until you can no longer see streaks of flour. The dough should be quite wet.

3. Spread the all-purpose (not self-rising) flour out on a small cookie sheet. With a spoon, scoop 8 evenly sized balls of dough into the flour, making sure they don't touch each other. With floured hands, coat each dough ball with flour and toss them gently from hand to hand to stir any excess flour. Place each floured dough ball into the prepared pan, right up next to the other. This will help the biscuits rise up, rather than spreading out.

4. Preheat the toaster oven to 380°F.

5. Transfer the cake pan to the air fryer oven, lowering it into the air fryer oven using a sling made of aluminum foil (fold a piece of aluminum foil into a strip about 2-inches wide by 24-inches long). Let the ends of the aluminum foil sling hang across the cake pan before returning to the air fryer oven.

6. Air-fry for 20 minutes. Check the biscuits a couple of times to make sure they are not getting too brown on top. If they are, re-arrange the aluminum foil strips to cover any brown parts. After 20 minutes, check the biscuits by inserting a toothpick into the center of the biscuits. It should come out clean. If it needs a little more time, continue to air-fry for a couple of extra minutes. Brush the tops of the biscuits with some melted butter and sprinkle a little more grated cheese on top if desired. Air-fry for another 2 minutes. Remove the cake pan from the air fryer oven using the aluminum sling. Let the biscuits cool for just a minute or two and then turn them out onto a plate and pull apart. Serve immediately.

Cherry Almond Scones

Servings: 12

Cooking Time: 25 Minutes

Ingredients:

- 2 3/4 cups all-purpose flour
- 1/2 cup sugar
- 1 tablespoon baking powder
- 3/4 teaspoon salt
- 1 cup dried cherries
- 1 cup slivered almonds
- 1/2 cup cold butter, sliced into tablespoons
- 2 large eggs
- 1/2 cup sour cream
- 1 teaspoon almond extract
- 1/2 teaspoon vanilla extract
- 1 tablespoon milk
- Coarse sugar

Directions:

1. Preheat the toaster oven to 375°F.
2. In a large mixer bowl, stir flour, sugar, baking powder and salt until blended.
3. Add butter pieces. Beat on MEDIUM speed until mixture is crumbly with some larger pieces of butter.
4. In a large mixer bowl on MEDIUM-HIGH speed, beat eggs, sour cream, almond extract and vanilla extract until blended.
5. Stir into flour mixture until mixture is blended and no longer dry. Lightly knead in cherries and almonds.
6. Divide dough in half. Form each into circles about 3/4-inch thick on parchment-lined baking sheet.
7. Brush each circle with milk and sprinkle tops with coarse sugar. Using a floured metal spatula, cut each circle into 6 wedges. Separate the wedges, leaving 1/2-inch between each wedge.
8. Bake for 20 to 25 minutes or until golden brown. Cool for 15 minutes before serving.

Strawberry Toast

Servings: 4

Cooking Time: 8 Minutes

Ingredients:

- 4 slices bread, ½-inch thick
- butter-flavored cooking spray
- 1 cup sliced strawberries
- 1 teaspoon sugar

Directions:

1. Spray one side of each bread slice with butter-flavored cooking spray. Lay slices sprayed side down.
2. Divide the strawberries among the bread slices.
3. Sprinkle evenly with the sugar and place in the air fryer oven in a single layer.
4. Air-fry at 390°F for 8 minutes. The bottom should look brown and crisp and the top should look glazed.

Hole In One

Servings: 1

Cooking Time: 7 Minutes

Ingredients:

- 1 slice bread
- 1 teaspoon soft butter
- 1 egg
- salt and pepper
- 1 tablespoon shredded Cheddar cheese
- 2 teaspoons diced ham

Directions:

1. Place a 6 x 6-inch baking dish inside air fryer oven and preheat fryer to 330°F.
2. Using a 2½-inch-diameter biscuit cutter, cut a hole in center of bread slice.
3. Spread softened butter on both sides of bread.
4. Lay bread slice in baking dish and crack egg into the hole. Sprinkle egg with salt and pepper to taste.
5. Air-fry for 5 minutes.
6. Turn toast over and top it with shredded cheese and diced ham.
7. Air-fry for 2 more minutes or until yolk is done to your liking.

Nacho Chips

Servings: 12

Cooking Time: 20 Minutes

Ingredients:

- ➢ 3 jalapeño peppers
- ➢ 4 6-inch flour tortillas
- ➢ 1 cup shredded low-fat Cheddar cheese

Directions:

1. Seed and cut the jalapeño peppers into thin rings. Arrange one-fourth of the rings on the tortilla. It's a good idea to wear gloves, since the peppers can sometimes cause skin irritation.

2. Place the tortilla in an oiled or nonstick 8½ × 8½ × 2-inch square baking (cake) pan. Sprinkle evenly with ¼ cup cheese.

3. BROIL for 5 minutes, or until the cheese is melted. Repeat the process for the remaining tortillas. Cut each into 6 wedges with a sharp knife or scissors.

French Toast

Servings: 4

Cooking Time: 40 Minutes

Ingredients:

- 2 eggs
- 1 cup skim milk or low-fat soy milk
- 1 tablespoon honey
- Salt
- 4 slices multigrain bread
- Vegetable oil

Directions:

1. Whisk together the eggs, milk, honey, and salt to taste in a shallow bowl. Add a bread slice to the mixture and let it soak for one minute. Carefully turn it over and let the liquid saturate the other side. With a spatula, place the bread slice in an oiled 6½ × 6½ × 2-inch square (cake) pan.

2. BROIL for 5 minutes, then turn carefully with a spatula and broil for another 5 minutes, or until golden brown. Repeat the soaking and broiling procedure for the remaining slices.

Egg-loaded Potato Skins

Servings: 4

Cooking Time: 55 Minutes

Ingredients:

- 2 large russet potatoes
- ½ teaspoon olive oil
- ½ cup Gruyère cheese, shredded and divided
- 4 large eggs
- ¼ cup heavy (whipping) cream, divided
- 1 scallion, both white and green parts, finely chopped
- Sea salt, for seasoning
- Freshly ground black pepper, for seasoning

Directions:

1. Preheat the toaster oven to 400°F on BAKE.

2. Prick the potatoes all over with a fork and rub with the olive oil.

3. Place the potatoes directly on the rack and bake for 40 minutes. The potatoes should be soft and tender, and the skin lightly browned. If not done, set the timer for 5 minutes more.

4. Take the potatoes out and set aside until cool enough to handle, about 10 minutes.

5. Cut the potatoes in half lengthwise and scoop out the flesh so that you have about ½-inch flesh and the intact skin. Place the potato halves in the air-fryer basket (placed on the baking tray) and sprinkle 2 tablespoons of cheese in each skin. Crack an egg into each potato half and spoon 1 tablespoon of cream over each egg. Sprinkle with scallion and lightly season with salt and pepper.

6. In position 1, bake for 15 minutes until the egg whites are set, and the yolks are still runny. If the eggs need more time, set the timer for 3 to 5 minutes more. Serve.

Sheet-pan Hash Browns

Servings: 2

Cooking Time: 60 Minutes

Ingredients:

- 1½ pounds Yukon Gold potatoes, unpeeled, shredded
- 3 tablespoons extra-virgin olive oil
- ½ teaspoon table salt
- ⅛ teaspoon pepper

Directions:

1. Adjust toaster oven rack to lowest position, select air-fry or convection function, and preheat the toaster oven to 450 degrees. Place potatoes in large bowl and cover with cold water. Let sit for 5 minutes.

2. Lift potatoes out of water, one handful at a time, and transfer to colander; discard water. Rinse and dry bowl. Place half of shredded potatoes in center of clean dish towel. Gather ends of towel and twist tightly to wring out excess moisture from potatoes. Transfer dried potatoes to now-empty bowl. Repeat with remaining potatoes.

3. Add oil, salt, and pepper to potatoes and toss to combine. Distribute potatoes in even layer on small rimmed baking sheet, but do not pack down. Cook until top of potatoes is spotty brown, 30 to 40 minutes, rotating sheet halfway through baking.

4. Remove sheet from oven. Using spatula, flip hash browns in sections. Return sheet to oven and continue to cook until spotty brown and dry, 10 to 15 minutes. Season with salt and pepper to taste. Serve.

Savory Salsa Cheese Rounds

Servings: 6

Cooking Time: 6 Minutes

Ingredients:

- ➢ 1 French baguette, cut to make 12
- ➢ 1-inch slices (rounds)
- ➢ ¼ cup olive oil
- ➢ 1 cup Tomato Salsa (recipe follows)
- ➢ ½ cup shredded low-fat mozzarella
- ➢ 2 tablespoons finely chopped fresh cilantro

Directions:

1. Brush both sides of each round with olive oil.

2. Spread one side of each slice with salsa and sprinkle each with mozzarella. Place the rounds in an oiled or nonstick 8½ × 8½ × 2-inch square baking (cake) pan.

3. BROIL for 6 minutes, or until the cheese is melted and the rounds are lightly browned. Garnish with the chopped cilantro and serve.

English Muffin Express Sandwich

Servings: 2

Cooking Time: 5 Minutes

Ingredients:

- 1 tablespoon mayonnaise
- 1 tablespoon chopped green onions, white and green portions
- ¼ teaspoon garlic powder
- 1 tablespoon unsalted butter, plus softened butter for spreading
- 2 large eggs
- Kosher salt and freshly ground black pepper
- 2 English muffins, split
- 2 slices Canadian bacon or thin, deli-style cooked ham
- 2 slices cheddar cheese

Directions:

1. Stir the mayonnaise, green onions, and garlic powder in a small bowl; set aside.

2. Melt 1 tablespoon butter in a small, nonstick skillet over medium heat. Whisk 1 egg in a small bowl and season with salt and pepper. Pour the egg into the skillet. Cook about 1 minute or until the egg is cooked on the bottom, gently turn the egg, and cook the second side. Remove the cooked egg from the skillet and keep warm. Repeat with the second egg.

3. Toast the English muffins in the toaster oven. Remove the toasted muffins and lightly spread the softened butter on the cut surface of each muffin. Place a slice of Canadian bacon and cheese on the bottom piece of each muffin. (Fold the cheese as necessary and do not allow the edges of the cheese to hang over the edges of the muffin.) Place the muffin, cheese-side up, in a baking pan. Heat on Toast or Broil for 1 to 2 minutes or until the cheese is melted.

4. Spread the top piece of each English muffin with the mayonnaise mixture.

5. Remove the cheese-topped English muffin from the toaster oven. Place the cooked egg on top of the melted cheese, folding to fit, as necessary. Top with the other piece of the English muffin, mayonnaise side down. Serve warm.

LUNCH AND DINNER

Pesto Pizza

Servings: 1

Cooking Time: 20 Minutes

Ingredients:

- Topping:
- ½ cup chopped fresh basil
- 1 tablespoon pine nuts (pignoli)
- 1 tablespoon olive oil
- 2 tablespoons shredded Parmesan cheese
- 1 garlic clove, minced
- ½ teaspoon dried oregano or 1 tablespoon chopped fresh oregano
- 1 plum tomato, chopped
- Salt and pepper to taste
- 1 9-inch ready-made pizza crust
- 2 tablespoons shredded low-fat mozzarella

Directions:

1. Preheat the toaster oven to 375° F.

2. Combine the topping ingredients in a small bowl.

3. Process the mixture in a blender or food processor until smooth. Spread the mixture on the pizza crust, then sprinkle with the mozzarella cheese. Place the pizza crust on the toaster oven rack.

4. BAKE for 20 minutes, or until the cheese is melted and the crust is brown.

Rosemary Lentils

Servings: 2

Cooking Time: 35 Minutes

Ingredients:

- ¼ cup lentils
- 1 tablespoon mashed Roasted Garlic
- 1 rosemary sprig
- 1 bay leaf
- Salt and freshly ground black pepper
- 2 tablespoons low-fat buttermilk
- 2 tablespoons tomato sauce

Directions:

1. Preheat the toaster oven to 400° F.

2. Combine the lentils, 1¼ cups water, garlic, rosemary sprig, and bay leaf in a 1-quart 8½ × 8½ × 4-inch ovenproof baking dish, stirring to blend well. Add the salt and pepper to taste. Cover with aluminum foil.

3. BAKE, covered, for 35 minutes, or until the lentils are tender. Remove the rosemary sprig and bay leaf and stir in the buttermilk and tomato sauce. Serve immediately.

Roasted Vegetable Gazpacho

Servings: 4

Cooking Time: 35 Minutes

Ingredients:

- ➤ Vegetables and seasonings:
- ➤ 1 bell pepper, thinly sliced
- ➤ ½ cup chopped celery
- ➤ ½ cup frozen or canned corn
- ➤ 1 medium onion, thinly sliced
- ➤ 1 small yellow squash, cut into 1-inch slices
- ➤ 1 small zucchini, cut into 1-inch slices
- ➤ 3 garlic cloves, chopped
- ➤ ½ teaspoon ground cumin
- ➤ 2 tablespoons olive oil
- ➤ Salt and freshly ground black pepper to taste
- ➤ 1 quart tomato juice
- ➤ 1 tablespoon lemon juice
- ➤ 3 tablespoons chopped fresh cilantro

Directions:

1. Preheat the toaster oven to 400°F.

2. Combine the vegetables and seasonings in an oiled or nonstick 8½ × 8½ × 2-inch square baking (cake) pan, mixing well.

3. BAKE, covered, for 25 minutes, or until the onions and celery are tender. Remove from the oven, uncover, and turn the vegetable pieces with tongs.

4. BROIL for 10 minutes, or until the vegetables are lightly browned. Remove from the oven and cool. Transfer to a large nonaluminum container and add the tomato juice, lemon juice, and cilantro. Adjust the seasonings.

5. Chill, covered, for several hours, preferably a day or two to enrich the flavor of the stock.

Sun-dried Tomato Pizza

Servings: 4

Cooking Time: 25 Minutes

Ingredients:

➢ Tomato mixture:

➢ 1 cup chopped sun-dried tomatoes

➢ 2 tablespoons tomato paste

➢ 2 tablespoons olive oil

➢ 2 tablespoons chopped onion

➢ 2 garlic cloves, minced

➢ 1 teaspoon dried oregano

➢ 1 teaspoon dried basil

➢ Salt and red pepper flakes to taste

➢ 1 9-inch ready-made pizza crust

➢ 1 5-ounce can mushrooms

➢ ¼ cup pitted and sliced black olives

➢ ½ cup shredded low-fat mozzarella cheese

Directions:

1. Combine the tomato mixture ingredients with ½ cup water in an 8½ × 8½ × 2-inch square baking (cake) pan.

2. BROIL for 8 minutes, or until the tomatoes are softened. Remove from the oven and cool for 5 minutes.

3. Process the mixture in a blender or food processor until well blended. Spread on the pizza crust and layer with the mushrooms, olives, and cheese.

4. BAKE at 400° F. for 25 minutes, or until the cheese is melted.

Crunchy Baked Chicken Tenders

Servings: 3-4

Cooking Time: 18 Minutes

Ingredients:

- 2/3 cup seasoned panko breadcrumbs
- 2/3 cup cheese crackers, crushed
- 2 teaspoons melted butter
- 2 large eggs, beaten
- Salt and pepper
- 1 1/2 pounds chicken tenders
- Barbecue sauce

Directions:

1. Preheat the toaster oven to 450°F. Spray the toaster oven baking pan with nonstick cooking spray.
2. In medium bowl, combine breadcrumbs, cheese cracker crumbs and butter.
3. In another medium bowl, mix eggs, salt and pepper.
4. Dip chicken tenders in eggs and dredge in breadcrumb mixture.
5. Place on pan.
6. Bake for 15 to 18 minutes, turning once. Serve with barbecue sauce for dipping.

French Onion Soup

Servings: 4

Cooking Time: 46 Minutes

Ingredients:

- ➤ 1 cup finely chopped onions
- ➤ 1 teaspoon toasted sesame oil
- ➤ 1 tablespoon vegetable oil
- ➤ 2 ½ cup dry white wine
- ➤ 3 teaspoons soy sauce
- ➤ ½ teaspoon garlic powder
- ➤ Freshly ground black pepper to taste
- ➤ 4 French bread rounds, sliced 1 inch thick
- ➤ 4 tablespoons grated Parmesan cheese
- ➤ 1 tablespoon chopped fresh parsley

Directions:

1. Place the onions, sesame oil, and vegetable oil in an 8½ × 8½ × 2-inch square baking (cake) pan.

2. BROIL for 10 minutes, stirring every 3 minutes until the onions are tender. Remove from the oven and transfer to a 1-quart 8½ × 8½ × 4-inch ovenproof baking dish. Add 2 cups water, the wine, and the soy sauce. Add the garlic powder and pepper and adjust the seasonings.

3. BAKE, covered, at 400° F. for 30 minutes. Remove from the oven, uncover, and add the 4 bread rounds, letting them float on top of the soup. Sprinkle each with 1 tablespoon Parmesan cheese.

4. BROIL, uncovered, for 6 minutes, or until the cheese is lightly browned. With tongs, transfer the bread rounds to 4 individual soup bowls. Ladle the soup on top of the bread rounds. Garnish with the parsley and serve immediately.

Zucchini Casserole

Servings: 4

Cooking Time: 37 Minutes

Ingredients:

- 4 small zucchini squashes, halved and quartered
- 2 plum tomatoes, quartered
- 1 8-ounce can tomato sauce
- 2 tablespoons chopped onion
- 2 garlic cloves, minced
- 1 tablespoon olive oil
- 1 tablespoon chopped fresh oregano
- 1 tablespoon chopped fresh basil
- 2 tablespoons pine nuts (pignoli)
- Salt and freshly ground black pepper to taste
- ½ cup shredded low-fat mozzarella cheese

Directions:

1. Preheat the toaster oven to 400° F.

2. Combine all the ingredients, except the mozzarella cheese, in a 1-quart 8½ × 8½ × 4-inch ovenproof baking dish. Cover with aluminum foil.

3. BAKE, covered, for 30 minutes, or until the zucchini is tender. Uncover and sprinkle the top with the cheese.

4. BROIL for 7 minutes, or until the cheese is melted and lightly browned.

Roasted Harissa Chicken + Vegetables

Servings: 4   Cooking Time: 30 Minutes

Ingredients:

- Nonstick cooking spray
- 1 medium zucchini, halved lengthwise and sliced crosswise ½ inch thick
- ½ large red onion, sliced ¼ inch thick
- 2 tablespoons olive oil
- Kosher salt and freshly ground black pepper
- 1 pound boneless, skinless chicken breasts, cut into 1-inch cubes
- ½ teaspoon ground cumin
- 1 clove garlic, minced
- 2 tablespoons harissa sauce or paste
- 1 tablespoon honey
- 2 tablespoons minced fresh cilantro
- 2 cups hot cooked rice
- Optional toppings: plain Greek yogurt or sour cream, sesame seeds (toasted or chopped), or dry-roasted peanuts

Directions:

1. Preheat the toaster oven to 400°F. Spray a 12 x 12-inch baking pan with nonstick cooking spray.

2. Place the zucchini and red onion in a medium bowl. Drizzle with 1 tablespoon olive oil and season with salt and pepper. Stir to coat the vegetables evenly. Arrange the vegetables in a single layer in the prepared baking pan. Roast, uncovered, for 10 minutes.

3. Place the chicken cubes in that same bowl. Drizzle with the remaining 1 tablespoon olive oil. Season with the cumin, garlic, salt, and pepper. Stir to coat the chicken evenly.

4. Stir the vegetables and move to one side of the pan. Arrange the chicken in a single layer on the other side of the pan. Roast for 10 minutes.

5. Blend the harissa and honey in a small bowl. Drizzle the sauce over the chicken and vegetables. Using a pastry brush, coat the chicken and vegetables evenly. Roast, uncovered, for an additional 8 to 10 minutes, or until the vegetables are tender and the chicken registers 165°F on a meat thermometer.

6. Spoon the chicken, vegetables, and any collected liquid onto a serving platter. Sprinkle with the cilantro. Serve the chicken and vegetables with the rice and, if desired, a dollop of plain Greek yogurt and a sprinkling of sesame seeds.

Baked Parsleyed Cheese Grits

Servings: 4

Cooking Time: 30 Minutes

Ingredients:

- ➤ 4 strips lean uncooked turkey bacon, cut in half
- ➤ 1 cup grits
- ➤ 2 cups skim or low-fat soy milk
- ➤ 1 egg
- ➤ ½ cup shredded Parmesan cheese
- ➤ 1 tablespoon chopped fresh parsley
- ➤ ½ teaspoon garlic powder
- ➤ Salt and butcher's pepper to taste

Directions:

1. Preheat the toaster oven to 350° F.
2. Layer an 8½ × 8½ × 2-inch square baking (cake) pan with the bacon strips.
3. Combine the remaining ingredients in a medium bowl and pour the mixture over the strips.
4. BAKE, uncovered, for 30 minutes, or until the grits are cooked. Cut into squares with a spatula and serve.

Broiled Chipotle Tilapia With Avocado Sauce

Servings: 2

Cooking Time: 10 Minutes

Ingredients:

- 1 small avocado, halved, pitted and peeled
- 3 tablespoons sour cream
- 1 teaspoon lime juice
- 2 1/2 teaspoons chipotle and roasted garlic seasoning, divided
- 1 tablespoon mayonnaise
- 1/2 pound tilapia fillets
- Chopped cilantro

Directions:

1. Using a chopper or small food processor, blend avocado, sour cream, lime juice and 1 1/2 teaspoons seasoning until smooth. Cover and refrigerate.
2. Spray toaster oven baking pan with nonstick cooking spray.
3. in small bowl, mix mayonnaise and remaining 1 teaspoon seasoning.
4. Brush mayonnaise mixture on both sides of tilapia fillets.
5. Place coated fish in pan.
6. Set toaster oven to BROIL. Broil fish for 10 minutes or until fish flakes with a fork.
7. Serve with avocado sauce and garnish with lime slices and cilantro, if desired.

Baked Picnic Pinto Beans

Servings: 4

Cooking Time: 40 Minutes

Ingredients:

- 1 tomato, peeled and finely chopped
- 2 15-ounce cans pinto beans, drained
- 6 lean turkey bacon strips, cooked, drained, and crumbled
- 1 cup good-quality dark beer or ale
- 3 tablespoons finely chopped onion
- 1 tablespoon ketchup
- 2 tablespoons molasses
- 1 teaspoon Dijon mustard
- 1 teaspoon Worcestershire sauce
- 1 teaspoon garlic powder
- Salt and butcher's pepper to taste

Directions:

1. Preheat the toaster oven to 375° F.

2. Peel the tomato by immersing it in boiling water for 1 minute. Remove with tongs and when cool enough to handle, pull the skin away with a sharp paring knife. Chop and place in a 1-quart 8½ × 8½ × 4-inch ovenproof baking dish. Add all the other ingredients, stirring to mix well. Adjust the seasonings to taste. Cover with aluminum foil.

3. BAKE, covered, for 40 minutes.

Fillets En Casserole

Servings: 4

Cooking Time: 20 Minutes

Ingredients:

- ½ cup multigrain bread crumbs
- 4 6-ounce fish fillets
- Sauce:
- 2 tablespoons white wine
- 1 teaspoon Worcestershire sauce
- 1 teaspoon lemon juice
- 1 tablespoon vegetable oil
- 1 teaspoon Dijon mustard
- Salt and freshly ground black pepper to taste
- 2 tablespoons capers

Directions:

1. Preheat the toaster oven to 400° F.
2. Layer the bottom of an oiled or nonstick 8½ × 8½ × 2-inch square baking (cake) pan with the bread crumbs and place the fillets on the crumbs.
3. Combine the sauce ingredients, mixing well, and spoon over the fillets. Sprinkle with the capers.
4. BAKE, covered, for 20 minutes, or until the fish flakes easily with a fork.

Kashaburgers

Servings: 4

Cooking Time: 50 Minutes

Ingredients:

- 1 cup kasha
- 2 tablespoons minced onion or scallions
- 1 tablespoon minced garlic
- ½ cup multigrain bread crumbs
- 1 egg
- ¼ teaspoon paprika
- ½ teaspoon chili powder
- ¼ teaspoon sesame oil
- 1 tablespoon vegetable oil
- Salt and freshly ground black pepper to taste

Directions:

1. Preheat the toaster oven to 400° F.
2. Combine 2 cups water and the kasha in a 1-quart 8½ × 8½ × 4-inch ovenproof baking dish.
3. BAKE, uncovered, for 30 minutes, or until the grains are cooked. Remove from the oven and add all the other ingredients, stirring to mix well. When the mixture is cooled, shape into 4 to 6 patties and place on a rack with a broiling pan underneath.
4. BROIL for 20 minutes, turn with a spatula, then broil for another 10 minutes, or until browned.

Nice + Easy Baked Macaroni + Cheese

Servings: 6

Cooking Time: 35 Minutes

Ingredients:

- Nonstick cooking spray
- 2 cups whole milk
- 3 ounces cream cheese
- ½ teaspoon kosher salt
- 1 clove garlic
- ¼ teaspoon freshly ground black pepper
- 8 ounces macaroni, uncooked
- 2 cups shredded cheddar cheese
- 2 tablespoons unsalted butter, melted
- ¼ cup grated Parmesan cheese
- 1 cup panko bread crumbs

Directions:

1. Preheat the toaster oven to 425°F. Spray an 11 x 7 x 2 ½-inch baking dish with nonstick cooking spray.

2. Place the milk, cream cheese, salt, garlic, and pepper into a blender. Blend until smooth.

3. Add macaroni to the prepared dish. Sprinkle with the cheddar cheese. Pour the milk mixture over all.

4. Combine the butter, Parmesan, and panko in a small bowl. Sprinkle the crumb mixture over the macaroni. Bake, uncovered, for 25 to 35 minutes or until the top is golden brown. Remove from the oven and let stand for at least 10 minutes.

FISH AND SEAFOOD

Fried Oysters

Servings: 12

Cooking Time: 8 Minutes

Ingredients:

- ➢ 1½ cups All-purpose flour
- ➢ 1½ cups Yellow cornmeal
- ➢ 1½ tablespoons Cajun dried seasoning blend
- ➢ 1¼ cups, plus more if needed Amber beer, pale ale, or IPA
- ➢ 12 Large shucked oysters, any liquid drained off
- ➢ Vegetable oil spray

Directions:

1. Preheat the toaster oven to 400°F.

2. Whisk ⅔ cup of the flour, ½ cup of the cornmeal, and the seasoning blend in a bowl until uniform. Set aside.

3. Whisk the remaining ⅓ cup flour and the remaining ½ cup cornmeal with the beer in a second bowl, adding more beer in dribs and drabs until the mixture is the consistency of pancake batter.

4. Using a fork, dip a shucked oyster in the beer batter, coating it thoroughly. Gently shake off any excess batter, then set the oyster in the dry mixture and turn gently to coat well and evenly. Set the coated oyster on a cutting board and continue dipping and coating the remainder of the oysters.

5. Coat the oysters with vegetable oil spray, then set them in the air fryer oven with as much air space between them as possible. Air-fry undisturbed for 8 minutes, or until lightly browned and crisp.

6. Use a nonstick-safe spatula to transfer the oysters to a wire rack. Cool for a couple of minutes before serving.

Shrimp Patties

Servings: 4

Cooking Time: 10 Minutes

Ingredients:

- ½ pound shelled and deveined raw shrimp
- ¼ cup chopped red bell pepper
- ¼ cup chopped green onion
- ¼ cup chopped celery
- 2 cups cooked sushi rice
- ½ teaspoon garlic powder
- ½ teaspoon Old Bay Seasoning
- ½ teaspoon salt
- 2 teaspoons Worcestershire sauce
- ½ cup plain breadcrumbs
- oil for misting or cooking spray

Directions:

1. Finely chop the shrimp. You can do this in a food processor, but it takes only a few pulses. Be careful not to overprocess into mush.

2. Place shrimp in a large bowl and add all other ingredients except the breadcrumbs and oil. Stir until well combined.

3. Preheat the toaster oven to 390°F.

4. Shape shrimp mixture into 8 patties, no more than ½-inch thick. Roll patties in breadcrumbs and mist with oil or cooking spray.

5. Place 4 shrimp patties in air fryer oven and air-fry at 390°F for 10 minutes, until shrimp cooks through and outside is crispy.

6. Repeat step 5 to cook remaining shrimp patties.

Blackened Red Snapper

Servings: 4

Cooking Time: 8 Minutes

Ingredients:

- 1½ teaspoons black pepper
- ¼ teaspoon thyme
- ¼ teaspoon garlic powder
- ⅛ teaspoon cayenne pepper
- 1 teaspoon olive oil
- 4 4-ounce red snapper fillet portions, skin on
- 4 thin slices lemon
- cooking spray

Directions:

1. Mix the spices and oil together to make a paste. Rub into both sides of the fish.

2. Spray air fryer oven with nonstick cooking spray and lay snapper steaks in air fryer oven, skin-side down.

3. Place a lemon slice on each piece of fish.

4. Air-fry at 390°F for 8 minutes. The fish will not flake when done, but it should be white through the center.

Oven-poached Salmon

Servings: 2

Cooking Time: 20 Minutes

Ingredients:

- Poaching liquid:
- 1 cup dry white wine
- 2 bay leaves
- 1 tablespoon mustard seed
- Salt and freshly ground black pepper to taste
- 2 6-ounce salmon steaks
- 2 tablespoons fresh watercress, rinsed, drained, and chopped (for serving hot)
- 1 lemon, cut into small wedges (for serving hot)
- Cucumber Sauce (recipe follows)

Directions:

1. Preheat the toaster oven to 350° F.

2. Combine the poaching liquid ingredients with 1 cup water in a small bowl and set aside.

3. Place the salmon steaks in an oiled or nonstick 8½ × 8½ × 2-inch square baking (cake) pan and pour enough poaching liquid over the steaks to barely cover them. Adjust the seasonings to taste.

4. BAKE, uncovered, for 20 minutes, or until the fish feels springy to the touch. Remove the bay leaves and serve the fish hot with watercress and lemon or cold with Cucumber Sauce.

Pecan-crusted Tilapia

Servings: 4

Cooking Time: 8 Minutes

Ingredients:

- 1 pound skinless, boneless tilapia filets
- ¼ cup butter, melted
- 1 teaspoon minced fresh or dried rosemary
- 1 cup finely chopped pecans
- 1 teaspoon sea salt
- ¼ teaspoon paprika
- 2 tablespoons chopped parsley
- 1 lemon, cut into wedges

Directions:

1. Pat the tilapia filets dry with paper towels.

2. Pour the melted butter over the filets and flip the filets to coat them completely.

3. In a medium bowl, mix together the rosemary, pecans, salt, and paprika.

4. Preheat the toaster oven to 350°F.

5. Place the tilapia filets into the air fryer oven and top with the pecan coating. Air-fry for 6 to 8 minutes. The fish should be firm to the touch and flake easily when fully cooked.

6. Remove the fish from the air fryer oven. Top the fish with chopped parsley and serve with lemon wedges.

Broiled Lemon Coconut Shrimp

Servings: 4

Cooking Time: 10 Minutes

Ingredients:

- ➢ Brushing mixture:
- ➢ 2 tablespoons lemon juice
- ➢ 4 tablespoons olive oil
- ➢ 1 tablespoon grated lemon zest
- ➢ Salt to taste
- ➢ 1 pound fresh shrimp, peeled, deveined, and butterflied
- ➢ ½ cup grated unsweetened coconut

Directions:

1. Combine the brushing mixture ingredients in a small bowl. Add the shrimp and toss to coat well. Set aside.

2. Place the coconut on a plate, spreading it out evenly.

3. Press each shrimp into the coconut, coating well on all sides. Place the shrimp in an 8½ × 8½ × 2-inch oiled or nonstick square (cake) pan.

4. BROIL the shrimp for 5 minutes, turn with tongs, and broil for 5 more minutes, or until browned lightly.

Stuffed Baked Red Snapper

Servings: 2

Cooking Time: 30 Minutes

Ingredients:

- ➢ Stuffing mixture:
- ➢ 12 medium shrimp, cooked, peeled, and chopped
- ➢ 2 tablespoons multigrain bread crumbs
- ➢ 1 teaspoon anchovy paste
- ➢ ¼ teaspoon paprika
- ➢ Salt to taste
- ➢ 2 6-ounce red snapper fillets
- ➢ 1 egg
- ➢ ½ cup fat-free half-and-half
- ➢ 2 tablespoons cooking sherry

Directions:

1. Preheat the toaster oven to 350° F.

2. Combine all the stuffing mixture ingredients in a medium bowl and place a mound of mixture on one end of each fillet. Fold over the other fillet end, skewering the edge with toothpicks.

3. Place the rolled fillets in an oiled or nonstick 8½ × 8½ × 2-inch square baking (cake) pan.

4. Whisk the egg in a small bowl until light in color, then whisk in the half-and-half and sherry. Pour over the fillets. Cover the pan with aluminum foil.

5. BAKE for 30 minutes.

Crunchy Clam Strips

Servings: 3

Cooking Time: 8 Minutes

Ingredients:

- ½ pound Clam strips, drained
- 1 Large egg, well beaten
- ½ cup All-purpose flour
- ½ cup Yellow cornmeal
- 1½ teaspoons Table salt
- 1½ teaspoons Ground black pepper
- Up to ¾ teaspoon Cayenne
- Vegetable oil spray

Directions:

1. Preheat the toaster oven to 400°F.

2. Toss the clam strips and beaten egg in a bowl until the clams are well coated.

3. Mix the flour, cornmeal, salt, pepper, and cayenne in a large zip-closed plastic bag until well combined. Using a flatware fork or small kitchen tongs, lift the clam strips one by one out of the egg, letting any excess egg slip back into the rest. Put the strips in the bag with the flour mixture. Once all the strips are in the bag, seal it until the strips are well coated.

4. Use kitchen tongs to pick out the clam strips and lay them on a cutting board (leaving any extra flour mixture in the bag to be discarded). Coat the strips on both sides with vegetable oil spray.

5. When the machine is at temperature, spread the clam strips in the air fryer oven in one layer. They may touch in places, but try to leave as much air space as possible around them. Air-fry undisturbed for 8 minutes, or until brown and crunchy.

6. Gently dump the contents of the air fryer oven onto a serving platter. Cool for just a minute or two before serving hot.

Beer-battered Cod

Servings: 3

Cooking Time: 12 Minutes

Ingredients:

- 1½ cups All-purpose flour
- 3 tablespoons Old Bay seasoning
- 1 Large egg(s)
- ¼ cup Amber beer, pale ale, or IPA
- 3 4-ounce skinless cod fillets
- Vegetable oil spray

Directions:

1. Preheat the toaster oven to 400°F.

2. Set up and fill two shallow soup plates or small pie plates on your counter: one with the flour, whisked with the Old Bay until well combined; and one with the egg(s), whisked with the beer until foamy and uniform.

3. Dip a piece of cod in the flour mixture, turning it to coat on all sides (not just the top and bottom). Gently shake off any excess flour and dip the fish in the egg mixture, turning it to coat. Let any excess egg mixture slip back into the rest, then set the fish back in the flour mixture and coat it again, then back in the egg mixture for a second wash, then back in the flour mixture for a third time. Coat the fish on all sides with vegetable oil spray and set it aside. "Batter" the remaining piece(s) of cod in the same way.

4. Set the coated cod fillets in the air fryer oven with as much space between them as possible. They should not touch. Air-fry undisturbed for 12 minutes, or until brown and crisp.

5. Use kitchen tongs to gently transfer the fish to a wire rack. Cool for only a couple of minutes before serving.

Almond-crusted Fish

Servings: 4

Cooking Time: 10 Minutes

Ingredients:

- 4 4-ounce fish fillets
- ¾ cup breadcrumbs
- ¼ cup sliced almonds, crushed
- 2 tablespoons lemon juice
- ⅛ teaspoon cayenne
- salt and pepper
- ¾ cup flour
- 1 egg, beaten with 1 tablespoon water
- oil for misting or cooking spray

Directions:

1. Split fish fillets lengthwise down the center to create 8 pieces.
2. Mix breadcrumbs and almonds together and set aside.
3. Mix the lemon juice and cayenne together. Brush on all sides of fish.
4. Season fish to taste with salt and pepper.
5. Place the flour on a sheet of wax paper.
6. Roll fillets in flour, dip in egg wash, and roll in the crumb mixture.
7. Mist both sides of fish with oil or cooking spray.
8. Spray air fryer oven and lay fillets inside.
9. Air-fry at 390°F for 5 minutes, turn fish over, and air-fry for an additional 5 minutes or until fish is done and flakes easily.

Coconut Shrimp

Servings: 4

Cooking Time: 15 Minutes

Ingredients:

- ¼ cup cassava flour
- 1 teaspoon sugar
- ¼ teaspoon black pepper
- ½ teaspoon salt
- 2 large eggs
- 1 cup shredded coconut flakes, unsweetened
- ½ pound deveined, tail-off large shrimp

Directions:

1. Preheat the toaster oven to 330°F. Spray the air fryer oven with olive oil spray. Set aside.
2. In a small bowl, mix the flour, sugar, pepper, and salt.
3. In a separate bowl, whisk the eggs.
4. In a third bowl, place the coconut flakes.
5. Place 1 shrimp at a time in the flour mixture, then wash with the eggs, and cover with coconut flakes.
6. Liberally spray the metal trivet that fits inside the air fryer oven with olive oil spray. Place the shrimp onto the metal trivet and air-fry for 15 minutes, flipping halfway through. Repeat until all shrimp are cooked.
7. Serve immediately with desired sauce.

Sweet Chili Shrimp

Servings: 4

Cooking Time: 6 Minutes

Ingredients:

- ➢ 1 pound jumbo shrimp, peeled and deveined
- ➢ ¼ cup sweet chili sauce
- ➢ 1 lime, zested and juiced
- ➢ 1 tablespoon soy sauce
- ➢ 1 tablespoon honey
- ➢ 1 tablespoon olive oil
- ➢ 1 large garlic clove, minced
- ➢ ½ teaspoon salt
- ➢ ¼ teaspoon pepper
- ➢ 1 green onion, thinly sliced, for garnish

Directions:

1. Place the shrimp in a large bowl. Whisk all the remaining ingredients except the green onion in a separate bowl.

2. Pour sauce over the shrimp and toss to coat.

3. Preheat the toaster Oven to 430°F.

4. Line the food tray with foil, place shrimp on the tray, then insert at top position in the preheated oven.

5. Select the Air Fry function, adjust time to 6 minutes, and press Start/Pause.

6. Remove shrimp and garnish with sliced green onions.

Fish Tacos With Jalapeño-lime Sauce

Servings: 4   Cooking Time: 7 Minutes

Ingredients:

- Fish Tacos
- 1 pound fish fillets
- ¼ teaspoon cumin
- ¼ teaspoon coriander
- ⅛ teaspoon ground red pepper
- 1 tablespoon lime zest
- ¼ teaspoon smoked paprika
- 1 teaspoon oil
- cooking spray
- 6–8 corn or flour tortillas (6-inch size)
- Jalapeño-Lime Sauce
- ½ cup sour cream
- 1 tablespoon lime juice
- ¼ teaspoon grated lime zest
- ½ teaspoon minced jalapeño (flesh only)
- ¼ teaspoon cumin
- Napa Cabbage Garnish
- 1 cup shredded Napa cabbage
- ¼ cup slivered red or green bell pepper
- ¼ cup slivered onion

Directions:

1. Slice the fish fillets into strips approximately ½-inch thick.

2. Put the strips into a sealable plastic bag along with the cumin, coriander, red pepper, lime zest, smoked paprika, and oil. Massage seasonings into the fish until evenly distributed.

3. Spray air fryer oven with nonstick cooking spray and place seasoned fish inside.

4. Air-fry at 390°F for approximately 5 minutes. Distribute fish. Cook an additional 2 minutes, until fish flakes easily.

5. While the fish is cooking, prepare the Jalapeño-Lime Sauce by mixing the sour cream, lime juice, lime zest, jalapeño, and cumin together to make a smooth sauce. Set aside.

6. Mix the cabbage, bell pepper, and onion together and set aside.

7. To warm refrigerated tortillas, wrap in damp paper towels and microwave for 30 to 60 seconds.

8. To serve, spoon some of fish into a warm tortilla. Add one or two tablespoons Napa Cabbage Garnish and drizzle with Jalapeño-Lime Sauce.

Quick Shrimp Scampi

Servings: 2

Cooking Time: 5 Minutes

Ingredients:

- 16 to 20 raw large shrimp, peeled, deveined and tails removed
- ½ cup white wine
- freshly ground black pepper
- ¼ cup + 1 tablespoon butter, divided
- 1 clove garlic, sliced
- 1 teaspoon olive oil
- salt, to taste
- juice of ½ lemon, to taste
- ¼ cup chopped fresh parsley

Directions:

1. Start by marinating the shrimp in the white wine and freshly ground black pepper for at least 30 minutes, or as long as 2 hours in the refrigerator.

2. Preheat the toaster oven to 400°F.

3. Melt ¼ cup of butter in a small saucepan on the stovetop. Add the garlic and let the butter simmer, but be sure to not let it burn.

4. Pour the shrimp and marinade into the air fryer oven, letting the marinade drain through to the bottom drawer. Drizzle the olive oil on the shrimp and season well with salt. Air-fry at 400°F for 3 minutes. Turn the shrimp over and pour the garlic butter over the shrimp. Air-fry for another 2 minutes.

5. Remove the shrimp from the air fryer oven and transfer them to a bowl. Squeeze lemon juice over all the shrimp and toss with the chopped parsley and remaining tablespoon of butter. Season to taste with salt and serve immediately.

POULTRY

Turkey Sausage Cassoulet

Servings: 4

Cooking Time: 52 Minutes

Ingredients:

- 3 turkey sausages
- 1 teaspoon olive oil
- ½ sweet onion
- 2 celery stalks, chopped
- 1 teaspoon minced garlic
- 2 (15-ounce) cans great northern beans, drained and rinsed
- 1(15-ounce) can fire-roasted tomatoes
- 1 small sweet potato, diced
- 1 teaspoon dried thyme
- 2 cups kale, chopped
- Sea salt, for seasoning
- Freshly ground black pepper, for seasoning

Directions:

1. Preheat the toaster oven to 375°F on AIR FRY for 5 minutes.
2. Place the air-fryer basket in the baking tray and place the sausages in the basket. Prick them all over with a fork.
3. In position 2, air fry for 12 minutes until cooked through. Set the sausages aside to cool until you can handle them. Then cut into ¼-inch slices.
4. Change the oven to BAKE at 375°F and place the rack in position 1.
5. Heat the oil in a small skillet over medium-high heat and sauté the onion, celery, and garlic until softened.
6. Transfer the cooked vegetables to a 1½-quart casserole dish and stir in the sausage, beans, tomatoes, sweet potato, and thyme. Cover with foil or a lid.
7. Bake for 35 to 40 minutes until tender and any liquid is absorbed. Take the casserole out and stir in the kale. Let it sit for 10 minutes to wilt.
8. Season with salt and pepper, and serve.

Chicken-fried Steak With Gravy

Servings: 2   Cooking Time: 16 Minutes

Ingredients:

- FOR THE STEAK
- Oil spray (hand-pumped)
- 1 cup all-purpose flour
- 1 teaspoon garlic powder
- 1 teaspoon onion powder
- 1 teaspoon smoked paprika
- 2 large eggs
- 2 (½-pound) cube steaks
- Sea salt, for seasoning
- Freshly ground black pepper, for seasoning
- FOR THE GRAVY
- 2 tablespoons salted butter
- 2 tablespoons all-purpose flour
- 1½ cups whole milk
- ¼ cup heavy (whipping) cream
- Sea salt, for seasoning
- Freshly ground black pepper, for seasoning

Directions:

1. To make the steak
2. Preheat the toaster oven to 400°F on AIR FRY for 5 minutes.
3. Place the air-fryer basket in the baking tray and spray it generously with the oil.
4. In a medium bowl, stir the flour, garlic powder, onion powder, and paprika until well blended.
5. In a medium bowl, beat the eggs and place them next to the flour.
6. Season the steaks all over with salt and pepper.
7. Dredge a steak in the egg and then in the flour mixture, making sure it is well coated. Shake off any excess flour.
8. Place the steak in the basket and repeat the process with the other steak.
9. Spray the tops of the steaks with the oil.
10. In position 2, air fry for 9 minutes until golden brown and crispy. Turn the steaks over, spray the second side with the oil, and air fry for an additional 7 minutes.
11. Set the steaks aside to rest for 5 minutes.
12. To make the gravy
13. While the steak is air frying, melt the butter in a medium saucepan over medium-high heat.
14. Whisk in the flour and cook for 2 minutes until lightly browned.
15. Whisk in the milk until the gravy is creamy and thick, about 5 minutes. Whisk in the cream and season with salt and pepper.
16. Serve the steak topped with the gravy.

Crispy Duck With Cherry Sauce

Servings: 2   Cooking Time: 33 Minutes

Ingredients:

- 1 whole duck (up to 5 pounds), split in half, back and rib bones removed
- 1 teaspoon olive oil
- salt and freshly ground black pepper
- Cherry Sauce:
- 1 tablespoon butter
- 1 shallot, minced
- ½ cup sherry
- ¾ cup cherry preserves 1 cup chicken stock
- 1 teaspoon white wine vinegar
- 1 teaspoon fresh thyme leaves
- salt and freshly ground black pepper

Directions:

1. Preheat the toaster oven to 400°F.

2. Trim some of the fat from the duck. Rub olive oil on the duck and season with salt and pepper. Place the duck halves in the air fryer oven, breast side up and facing the center of the air fryer oven.

3. Air-fry the duck for 20 minutes. Turn the duck over and air-fry for another 6 minutes.

4. While duck is air-frying, make the cherry sauce. Melt the butter in a large sauté pan. Add the shallot and sauté until it is just starting to brown – about 2 to 3 minutes. Add the sherry and deglaze the pan by scraping up any brown bits from the bottom of the pan. Simmer the liquid for a few minutes, until it has reduced by half. Add the cherry preserves, chicken stock and white wine vinegar. Whisk well to combine all the ingredients. Simmer the sauce until it thickens and coats the back of a spoon – about 5 to 7 minutes. Season with salt and pepper and stir in the fresh thyme leaves.

5. When the air fryer oven timer goes off, spoon some cherry sauce over the duck and continue to air-fry at 400°F for 4 more minutes. Then, turn the duck halves back over so that the breast side is facing up. Spoon more cherry sauce over the top of the duck, covering the skin completely. Air-fry for 3 more minutes and then remove the duck to a plate to rest for a few minutes.

6. Serve the duck in halves, or cut each piece in half again for a smaller serving. Spoon any additional sauce over the duck or serve it on the side.

Chicken Potpie

Servings: 4

Cooking Time: 48 Minutes

Ingredients:

- Pie filling:
- 1 tablespoon unbleached flour
- ½ cup evaporated skim milk
- 4 skinless, boneless chicken thighs, cut into 1-inch cubes
- 1 cup potatoes, peeled and cut into ½-inch pieces
- ½ cup frozen green peas
- ½ cup thinly sliced carrot
- 2 tablespoons chopped onion
- ½ cup chopped celery
- 1 teaspoon garlic powder
- Salt and freshly ground black pepper to taste
- 8 sheets phyllo pastry, thawed Olive oil

Directions:

1. Preheat the toaster oven to 400° F.

2. Whisk the flour into the milk until smooth in a 1-quart 8½ × 8½ × 4-inch ovenproof baking dish. Add the remaining filling ingredients and mix well. Adjust the seasonings to taste. Cover the dish with aluminum foil.

3. BAKE for 40 minutes, or until the carrot, potatoes, and celery are tender. Remove from the oven and uncover.

4. Place one sheet of phyllo pastry on top of the baked pie-filling mixture, bending the edges to fit the shape of the baking dish. Brush the sheet with olive oil. Add another sheet on top of it and brush with oil. Continue adding the remaining sheets, brushing each one, until the crust is completed. Brush the top with oil.

5. BAKE for 6 minutes, or until the phyllo pastry is browned.

Chicken Fajitas

Servings: 4

Cooking Time: 15 Minutes

Ingredients:

- FOR THE FAJITAS
- ½ teaspoon ground cumin
- ½ teaspoon garlic powder
- ¼ teaspoon smoked paprika
- ¼ teaspoon onion powder
- ¼ teaspoon chili powder
- 1 pound boneless, skinless chicken breast, cut into ¼-inch strips
- 1 red bell pepper, cut into thin slices
- 1 green bell pepper, cut into thin slices
- 1 small red onion, cut into thin slices
- 2 tablespoons olive oil
- 8 (6-inch) tortillas
- OPTIONAL TOPPINGS
- Salsa
- Sour cream
- Pickled jalapeños
- Shredded lettuce

Directions:

1. Preheat the toaster oven to 375°F on AIR FRY for 5 minutes.

2. Place the air-fryer basket in the baking tray.

3. In a large bowl, stir the cumin, garlic powder, paprika, onion powder, and chili powder until well mixed. Add the chicken, bell peppers, onion, and oil, and toss to coat evenly.

4. Spread the chicken and veggies on the baking sheet.

5. In position 2, air fry for 15 minutes, tossing them halfway through, until cooked and the vegetables are lightly browned.

6. Serve tucked into the tortillas with your favorite toppings.

Apricot Glazed Chicken Thighs

Servings: 2

Cooking Time: 22 Minutes

Ingredients:

- 4 bone-in chicken thighs (about 2 pounds)
- olive oil
- 1 teaspoon salt
- ¼ teaspoon freshly ground black pepper
- ½ teaspoon onion powder
- ¾ cup apricot preserves 1½ tablespoons Dijon mustard
- ½ teaspoon dried thyme
- 1 teaspoon soy sauce
- fresh thyme leaves, for garnish

Directions:

1. Preheat the toaster oven to 380°F.

2. Brush or spray both the air fryer oven and the chicken with the olive oil. Combine the salt, pepper and onion powder and season both sides of the chicken with the spice mixture.

3. Place the seasoned chicken thighs, skin side down in the air fryer oven. Air-fry for 10 minutes.

4. While chicken is cooking, make the glaze by combining the apricot preserves, Dijon mustard, thyme and soy sauce in a small bowl.

5. When the time is up on the air fryer oven, spoon half of the apricot glaze over the chicken thighs and air-fry for 2 minutes. Then flip the chicken thighs over so that the skin side is facing up and air-fry for an additional 8 minutes. Finally, spoon and spread the rest of the glaze evenly over the chicken thighs and air-fry for a final 2 minutes. Transfer the chicken to a serving platter and sprinkle the fresh thyme leaves on top.

Chicken Pot Pie

Servings: 4

Cooking Time: 65 Minutes

Ingredients:

- ¼ cup salted butter
- 1 small sweet onion, chopped
- 1 carrot, chopped
- 1 teaspoon minced garlic
- ¼ cup all-purpose flour
- 1 cup low-sodium chicken broth
- ¼ cup heavy (whipping) cream
- 2 cups diced store-bought rotisserie chicken
- 1 cup frozen peas
- Sea salt, for seasoning
- Freshly ground black pepper, for seasoning
- 1 unbaked store-bought pie crust

Directions:

1. Place the rack in position 1 and preheat the toaster oven to 350°F on BAKE for 5 minutes.

2. Melt the butter in a large saucepan over medium-high heat. Sauté the onion, carrot, and garlic until softened, about 12 minutes. Whisk in the flour to form a thick paste and whisk for 1 minute to cook.

3. Add the broth and whisk until thickened, about 2 minutes. Add the heavy cream, whisking to combine. Add the chicken and peas, and season with salt and pepper.

4. Transfer the filling to a 1½-quart casserole dish and top with the pie crust, tucking the edges into the sides of the casserole dish to completely enclose the filling. Cut 4 or 5 slits in the top of the crust.

5. Bake for 50 minutes until the crust is golden brown and the filling is bubbly. Serve.

Chicken Hand Pies

Servings: 8

Cooking Time: 10 Minutes

Ingredients:

- ¾ cup chicken broth
- ¾ cup frozen mixed peas and carrots
- 1 cup cooked chicken, chopped
- 1 tablespoon cornstarch
- 1 tablespoon milk
- salt and pepper
- 1 8-count can organic flaky biscuits
- oil for misting or cooking spray

Directions:

1. In a medium saucepan, bring chicken broth to a boil. Stir in the frozen peas and carrots and air-fry for 5 minutes over medium heat. Stir in chicken.

2. Mix the cornstarch into the milk until it dissolves. Stir it into the simmering chicken broth mixture and cook just until thickened.

3. Remove from heat, add salt and pepper to taste, and let cool slightly.

4. Lay biscuits out on wax paper. Peel each biscuit apart in the middle to make 2 rounds so you have 16 rounds total. Using your hands or a rolling pin, flatten each biscuit round slightly to make it larger and thinner.

5. Divide chicken filling among 8 of the biscuit rounds. Place remaining biscuit rounds on top and press edges all around. Use the tines of a fork to crimp biscuit edges and make sure they are sealed well.

6. Spray both sides lightly with oil or cooking spray.

7. Cook in a single layer, 4 at a time, at 330°F for 10 minutes or until biscuit dough is cooked through and golden brown.

Chicken Cordon Bleu

Servings: 4

Cooking Time: 25 Minutes

Ingredients:

- Oil spray (hand-pumped)
- 4 (4-ounce) chicken breasts
- 4 teaspoons Dijon mustard
- 4 slices Gruyère cheese
- 4 slices lean ham
- 1 cup all-purpose flour
- 2 large eggs
- 1 cup bread crumbs
- ½ cup Parmesan cheese

Directions:

1. Preheat the toaster oven to 350°F on AIR FRY for 5 minutes.
2. Place the air-fryer basket in the baking tray and generously spray it with the oil.
3. Place a chicken breast flat on a clean work surface and cut along the length of the breast, almost in half, holding the knife parallel to the counter. Open the breast up like a book and place it between two pieces of plastic wrap. Pound the chicken breast to about ¼-inch thick with a rolling pin or mallet. Repeat with the remaining breasts.
4. Spread the mustard on each breast, place a piece of cheese and ham in the center, and fold the sides of the breast over the cheese and ham. Roll the breast up from the unfolded sides to form a sealed packet. Secure with a toothpick.
5. Repeat with the remaining breasts.
6. Sprinkle the flour on a plate and set it on your work surface.
7. In a small bowl, whisk the eggs until well beaten and place next to the flour.
8. In a medium bowl, stir the bread crumbs and Parmesan and place next to the eggs.
9. Dredge the chicken rolls in the flour, then egg, then the bread crumb mixture, making sure they are completely breaded.
10. Arrange the chicken in the basket and spray lightly all over with the oil.
11. In position 2, air fry for 25 minutes, turning halfway through, until golden brown. Serve.

Curry Powder

Servings: 1

Cooking Time: 5 Minutes

Ingredients:

- ½ cup coriander seeds
- 2 tablespoons ground cumin
- 2 tablespoons black peppercorns
- 1 tablespoon sesame seeds
- 1 tablespoon cardamom seeds, extracted from the pods
- 2 small dried chili peppers
- 3 tablespoons turmeric
- 2 tablespoons ground ginger

Directions:

1. Combine the coriander seeds, cumin, peppercorns, sesame seeds, cardamom seeds, and chili peppers in an oiled or nonstick 8½ × 8½ × 2-inch square baking (cake) pan.

2. TOAST once, then turn with tongs and toast again, or continue toasting and turning until evenly toasted. Cool and grind the spices in a blender until the mixture becomes a powder. Add the turmeric and ground ginger and mix well. Store in a covered container in the refrigerator.

Jerk Turkey Meatballs

Servings: 7

Cooking Time: 8 Minutes

Ingredients:

- 1 pound lean ground turkey
- ¼ cup chopped onion
- 1 teaspoon minced garlic
- ½ teaspoon dried thyme
- ¼ teaspoon ground cinnamon
- 1 teaspoon cayenne pepper
- ½ teaspoon paprika
- ½ teaspoon salt
- ⅛ teaspoon black pepper
- ¼ teaspoon red pepper flakes
- 2 teaspoons brown sugar
- 1 large egg, whisked
- ⅓ cup panko breadcrumbs
- 2⅓ cups cooked brown Jasmine rice
- 2 green onions, chopped
- ¾ cup sweet onion dressing

Directions:

1. Preheat the toaster oven to 350°F.

2. In a medium bowl, mix the ground turkey with the onion, garlic, thyme, cinnamon, cayenne pepper, paprika, salt, pepper, red pepper flakes, and brown sugar. Add the whisked egg and stir in the breadcrumbs until the turkey starts to hold together.

3. Using a 1-ounce scoop, portion the turkey into meatballs. You should get about 28 meatballs.

4. Spray the air fryer oven with olive oil spray.

5. Place the meatballs into the air fryer oven and air-fry for 5 minutes, rotate the meatball, and cook another 2 to 4 minutes (or until the internal temperature of the meatballs reaches 165°F).

6. Remove the meatballs from the air fryer oven and repeat for the remaining meatballs.

7. Serve warm over a bed of rice with chopped green onions and spicy Caribbean jerk dressing.

Fried Chicken

Servings: 4	Cooking Time: 40 Minutes

Ingredients:

- 12 skin-on chicken drumsticks
- 1 cup buttermilk
- 1½ cups all-purpose flour
- 1 tablespoon smoked paprika
- ¾ teaspoon celery salt
- ¾ teaspoon dried mustard
- ½ teaspoon garlic powder
- ½ teaspoon freshly ground black pepper
- ½ teaspoon sea salt
- ½ teaspoon dried thyme
- ¼ teaspoon dried oregano
- 4 large eggs
- Oil spray (hand-pumped)

Directions:

1. Place the chicken and buttermilk in a medium bowl, cover, and refrigerate for at least 1 hour, up to overnight.

2. Preheat the toaster oven to 375°F on **AIR FRY** for 5 minutes.

3. In a large bowl, stir the flour, paprika, celery salt, mustard, garlic powder, pepper, salt, thyme, and oregano until well mixed.

4. Beat the eggs until frothy in a medium bowl and set them beside the flour.

5. Place the air-fryer basket in the baking tray and generously spray it with the oil.

6. Dredge a chicken drumstick in the flour, then the eggs, and then in the flour again, thickly coating it, and place the drumstick in the basket. Repeat with 5 more drumsticks and spray them all lightly with the oil on all sides.

7. In position 2, air fry for 20 minutes, turning halfway through, until golden brown and crispy with an internal temperature of 165°F.

8. Repeat with the remaining chicken, covering the cooked chicken loosely with foil to keep it warm. Serve.

Poblano Bake

Servings: 4

Cooking Time: 11 Minutes

Ingredients:

- 2 large poblano peppers (approx. 5½ inches long excluding stem)
- ¾ pound ground turkey, raw
- ¾ cup cooked brown rice
- 1 teaspoon chile powder
- ½ teaspoon ground cumin
- ½ teaspoon garlic powder
- 4 ounces sharp Cheddar cheese, grated
- 1 8-ounce jar salsa, warmed

Directions:

1. Slice each pepper in half lengthwise so that you have four wide, flat pepper halves.
2. Remove seeds and membrane and discard. Rinse inside and out.
3. In a large bowl, combine turkey, rice, chile powder, cumin, and garlic powder. Mix well.
4. Divide turkey filling into 4 portions and stuff one into each of the 4 pepper halves. Press lightly to pack down.
5. Place 2 pepper halves in air fryer oven and air-fry at 390°F for 10 minutes or until turkey is well done.
6. Top each pepper half with ¼ of the grated cheese. Cook 1 more minute or just until cheese melts.
7. Repeat steps 5 and 6 to cook remaining pepper halves.
8. To serve, place each pepper half on a plate and top with ¼ cup warm salsa.

Chicken Souvlaki Gyros

Servings: 4

Cooking Time: 18 Minutes

Ingredients:

- ¼ cup extra-virgin olive oil
- 1 clove garlic, crushed
- 1 tablespoon Italian seasoning
- ½ teaspoon paprika
- ½ lemon, sliced
- ¼ teaspoon salt
- 1 pound boneless, skinless chicken breasts
- 4 whole-grain pita breads
- 1 cup shredded lettuce
- ½ cup chopped tomatoes
- ¼ cup chopped red onion
- ¼ cup cucumber yogurt sauce

Directions:

1. In a large resealable plastic bag, combine the olive oil, garlic, Italian seasoning, paprika, lemon, and salt. Add the chicken to the bag and secure shut. Vigorously shake until all the ingredients are combined. Set in the fridge for 2 hours to marinate.

2. When ready to cook, preheat the toaster oven to 360°F.

3. Liberally spray the air fryer oven with olive oil mist. Remove the chicken from the bag and discard the leftover marinade. Place the chicken into the air fryer oven, allowing enough room between the chicken breasts to flip.

4. Air-fry for 10 minutes, flip, and cook another 8 minutes.

5. Remove the chicken from the air fryer oven when it has cooked (or the internal temperature of the chicken reaches 165°F). Let rest 5 minutes. Then thinly slice the chicken into strips.

6. Assemble the gyros by placing the pita bread on a flat surface and topping with chicken, lettuce, tomatoes, onion, and a drizzle of yogurt sauce.

7. Serve warm.

SNACKS APPETIZERS AND SIDES

Skinny Fries

Servings: 2

Cooking Time: 15 Minutes

Ingredients:

- ➤ 2 to 3 russet potatoes, peeled and cut into ¼-inch sticks
- ➤ 2 to 3 teaspoons olive or vegetable oil
- ➤ salt

Directions:

1. Cut the potatoes into ¼-inch strips. (A mandolin with a julienne blade is really helpful here.) Rinse the potatoes with cold water several times and let them soak in cold water for at least 10 minutes or as long as overnight.

2. Preheat the toaster oven to 380°F.

3. Drain and dry the potato sticks really well, using a clean kitchen towel. Toss the fries with the oil in a bowl and then air-fry the fries in two batches at 380°F for 15 minutes.

4. Add the first batch of French fries back into the air fryer oven with the finishing batch and let everything warm through for a few minutes. As soon as the fries are done, season them with salt and transfer to a plate. Serve them warm with ketchup or your favorite dip.

Crispy Chili Kale Chips

Servings: 4

Cooking Time: 10 Minutes

Ingredients:

➢ 2 cups kale, stemmed and torn into 2-inch pieces

➢ 1 tablespoon extra-virgin olive oil

➢ ½ teaspoon chipotle chili powder

➢ Sea salt, for seasoning

Directions:

1. Preheat the toaster oven to 350°F on AIR FRY for 5 minutes.

2. Dry the kale with paper towels. Transfer the kale to a medium bowl and add the olive oil and chili powder. Toss the kale using your hands to evenly coat the leaves with the oil.

3. Place the air-fryer basket in the baking sheet and spread the kale in a single layer in the basket. You might have to cook two batches.

4. Air fry in position 2 for 5 minutes, until the leaves are crispy.

5. Transfer the kale chips to a large bowl and repeat with the remaining kale. Season the chips with salt and serve immediately.

Sesame Green Beans

Servings: 4

Cooking Time: 8 Minutes

Ingredients:

- 1 pound green beans, stems trimmed
- 1 tablespoon olive oil
- 1 teaspoon sesame oil
- 1 tablespoon sesame seeds
- Pinch sea salt

Directions:

1. Preheat the toaster oven to 350°F on AIR FRY for 5 minutes.
2. In a large bowl, toss the green beans, olive oil, and sesame oil.
3. Place the air-fryer basket in the baking tray and spread the beans in the basket.
4. Place the tray in position 2 and air fry for 8 minutes, shaking the basket at the halfway point. The beans should be lightly golden and fragrant.
5. Transfer the beans to a serving plate and serve topped with the sesame seeds and seasoned with salt.

Portobello Mushroom Bacon

Servings: 4

Cooking Time: 15 Minutes

Ingredients:

- 2 tablespoons light olive oil
- 2 tablespoons soy sauce
- 1 tablespoon pure maple syrup
- ½ teaspoon liquid smoke
- 1 teaspoon smoked paprika
- ¼ teaspoon red pepper flakes
- ¼ teaspoon pepper
- 2 portobello mushrooms, sliced into ⅛-inch-wide strips

Directions:

1. Whisk the olive oil, soy sauce, maple syrup, liquid smoke, smoked paprika, red pepper flakes, and pepper in a large bowl. Add the mushroom slices and toss to coat.
2. Preheat the toaster oven to 350°F.
3. Place the mushroom slices in the fry basket in an even layer, then insert the basket at mid position in the preheated oven.
4. Select the Air Fry and Shake functions, adjust time to 15 minutes, and press Start/Pause.
5. Flip mushroom slices halfway through cooking. The Shake Reminder will let you know when.
6. Remove when mushrooms are crispy.

Creamy Crab Dip

Servings: 4

Cooking Time: 20 Minutes

Ingredients:

- 6 ounces cream cheese, room temperature
- ½ cup sour cream
- ½ cup grated Parmesan cheese
- ½ cup shredded cheddar cheese
- Juice of ½ lemon
- ½ teaspoon garlic powder
- Dash hot sauce
- 1 (6-ounce) can crab meat, drained
- Sea salt, for seasoning
- Freshly ground black pepper, for seasoning
- Baguette, cut into ¼-inch-wide rounds, for serving

Directions:

1. Place the rack on position 1 and preheat the toaster oven on BAKE to 400°F for 5 minutes.
2. In a medium bowl, stir the cream cheese, sour cream, Parmesan, cheddar, lemon juice, garlic powder, and hot sauce until well blended.
3. Fold in the crab and season with salt and pepper.
4. Spoon the dip into a shallow heatproof 4-cup bowl.
5. Bake for 20 minutes until golden and bubbling.
6. Serve with baguette slices.

French Fries

Servings: 4

Cooking Time: 40 Minutes

Ingredients:

- 1 pound russet potatoes, scrubbed
- 2 tablespoons olive oil
- Sea salt, for seasoning
- Oil spray (hand-pumped)

Directions:

1. Cut the potatoes lengthwise into ¼-inch-wide batons (fries). Place the fries in a large bowl and cover them with cold water and set aside in the refrigerator for 1 hour.

2. Preheat the toaster oven on AIR FRY to 375°F for 5 minutes.

3. Drain the fries and pat them thoroughly with paper towels to get them as dry as possible.

4. Place the fries in a large bowl and add the olive oil. Generously season with salt.

5. Place the air-fryer basket in the baking sheet and generously spray it with oil.

6. Spread the fries in a single layer in the basket. You will have to do this in two batches. Cover the first batch loosely with foil to keep it warm while you cook the second batch.

7. In position 2, air fry for 10 minutes, then toss and cook for an additional 5 minutes until golden and crispy. If the fries are not crispy enough, cook for 5 additional minutes.

8. Repeat with the remaining fries. Serve immediately.

Beef Satay With Peanut Dipping Sauce

Servings: 4

Cooking Time: 60 Minutes

Ingredients:

- SKEWERS
- 1 pound flank steak, trimmed
- 2 tablespoons soy sauce
- 2 tablespoons vegetable oil
- 2 tablespoons packed dark brown sugar
- 2 tablespoons minced fresh cilantro
- 2 scallions, sliced thin
- 1½ tablespoons ketchup
- 1 garlic clove, minced
- ½ teaspoon sriracha
- SPICY PEANUT DIPPING SAUCE
- ¼ cup peanut butter (creamy or chunky)
- 2 tablespoons hot water, plus extra as needed
- 1½ tablespoons lime juice
- 1 scallion, sliced thin
- 1 tablespoon ketchup
- 1½ teaspoons soy sauce
- 1½ teaspoons packed dark brown sugar
- 1½ teaspoons minced fresh cilantro
- ¾ teaspoon sriracha
- 1 garlic clove, minced

Directions:

1. FOR THE SKEWERS: Slice beef against grain ¼ inch thick (you should have at least 20 slices).

2. Combine soy sauce, oil, sugar, cilantro, scallions, ketchup, garlic, and sriracha in medium bowl; add beef; and toss to combine. Cover and refrigerate for 15 minutes. Weave 1 beef slice evenly onto each skewer, leaving at least 1 inch at bottom of skewer exposed (Skewers can be refrigerated for up to 24 hours.)

3. FOR THE SPICY PEANUT DIPPING SAUCE: Whisk peanut butter and hot water together in medium bowl. Stir in lime juice, scallion, ketchup, soy sauce, sugar, cilantro, sriracha, and garlic. Adjust consistency with extra hot water as needed; set aside for serving.

4. Adjust toaster oven rack to middle position, select broiler function, and heat broiler. Set small wire rack in aluminum foil–lined small rimmed baking sheet and spray rack with vegetable oil spray. Arrange skewers in two rows across width of prepared rack with all exposed skewer ends facing center of rack. Cover skewer ends in center of sheet with strip of foil and secure by crimping tightly at edges. Broil skewers until beef is no longer pink on top, 2 to 3 minutes. Flip skewers and continue to broil until beef is fully cooked and spotty brown, 4 to 6 minutes. Serve with peanut sauce.

Apple Rollups

Servings: 8

Cooking Time: 5 Minutes

Ingredients:

- ➢ 8 slices whole wheat sandwich bread
- ➢ 4 ounces Colby Jack cheese, grated
- ➢ ½ small apple, chopped
- ➢ 2 tablespoons butter, melted

Directions:

1. Remove crusts from bread and flatten the slices with rolling pin. Don't be gentle. Press hard so that bread will be very thin.

2. Top bread slices with cheese and chopped apple, dividing the ingredients evenly.

3. Roll up each slice tightly and secure each with one or two toothpicks.

4. Brush outside of rolls with melted butter.

5. Place in air fryer oven and air-fry at 390°F for 5 minutes, until outside is crisp and nicely browned.

Sweet Plantain Chips

Servings: 4

Cooking Time: 11 Minutes

Ingredients:

- ➢ 2 Very ripe plantain(s), peeled and sliced into 1-inch pieces
- ➢ Vegetable oil spray
- ➢ 3 tablespoons Maple syrup
- ➢ For garnishing Coarse sea salt or kosher salt

Directions:

1. Pour about ½ cup water into the bottom of your air fryer oven or into a metal tray on a lower rack in some models. Preheat the toaster oven to 400°F.

2. Put the plantain pieces in a bowl, coat them with vegetable oil spray, and toss gently, spraying at least one more time and tossing repeatedly, until the pieces are well coated.

3. When the machine is at temperature, arrange the plantain pieces in the air fryer oven in one layer. Air-fry undisturbed for 5 minutes.

4. Remove the pan from the machine and spray the back of a metal spatula with vegetable oil spray. Use the spatula to press down on the plantain pieces, spraying it again as needed, to flatten the pieces to about half their original height. Brush the plantain pieces with maple syrup, then return the pan to the machine and continue air-frying undisturbed for 6 minutes, or until the plantain pieces are soft and caramelized.

5. Use kitchen tongs to transfer the pieces to a serving platter. Sprinkle the pieces with salt and cool for a couple of minutes before serving. Or cool to room temperature before serving, about 1 hour.

Shrimp Pirogues

Servings: 8

Cooking Time: 5 Minutes

Ingredients:

- 12 ounces small, peeled, and deveined raw shrimp
- 3 ounces cream cheese, room temperature
- 2 tablespoons plain yogurt
- 1 teaspoon lemon juice
- 1 teaspoon dried dill weed, crushed
- salt
- 4 small hothouse cucumbers, each approximately 6 inches long

Directions:

1. Pour 4 tablespoons water in bottom of air fryer oven.

2. Place shrimp in air fryer oven in single layer and air-fry at 390°F for 5 minutes, just until done. Watch carefully because shrimp cooks quickly, and overcooking makes it tough.

3. Chop shrimp into small pieces, no larger than ½ inch. Refrigerate while mixing the remaining ingredients.

4. With a fork, mash and whip the cream cheese until smooth.

5. Stir in the yogurt and beat until smooth. Stir in lemon juice, dill weed, and chopped shrimp.

6. Taste for seasoning. If needed, add ¼ to ½ teaspoon salt to suit your taste.

7. Store in refrigerator until serving time.

8. When ready to serve, wash and dry cucumbers and split them lengthwise. Scoop out the seeds and turn cucumbers upside down on paper towels to drain for 10 minutes.

9. Just before filling, wipe centers of cucumbers dry. Spoon the shrimp mixture into the pirogues and cut in half crosswise. Serve immediately.

Baked Spinach + Artichoke Dip

Servings: 5

Cooking Time: 40 Minutes

Ingredients:

- Nonstick cooking spray
- 2 tablespoons unsalted butter
- ½ medium onion, chopped
- 2 cloves garlic, minced
- 5 ounces frozen, chopped loose-pack spinach (about 1 ¾ cups), thawed and squeezed dry
- 1 (13.75-ounce) can quartered artichoke hearts, drained and chopped
- 1 (8-ounce) package cream cheese, cut into cubes and softened
- ½ cup mayonnaise
- Kosher salt and freshly ground black pepper
- 2 cups shredded Colby Jack or Mexican blend cheese
- ¾ cup shredded Parmesan cheese
- Tortilla chips, pita bread triangles, carrot or celery sticks, broccoli or cauliflower florets, for dipping

Directions:

1. Preheat the toaster oven to 350°F. Spray a 2-quart casserole dish with nonstick cooking spray.

2. Melt the butter in a large skillet over medium-high heat. Add the onion and cook, stirring frequently, until tender, 3 to 5 minutes. Add the garlic and cook, stirring frequently, for 30 seconds. Remove from the heat.

3. Stir in the spinach, artichokes, cream cheese, and mayonnaise. Season with salt and pepper. Blend in the Colby Jack and Parmesan cheeses. Spoon the mixture into the prepared casserole dish. Cover and bake for 20 minutes. Stir the dip and bake, covered, for an additional 10 to 15 minutes, or until hot and melted. Serve with any of the dipping choices.

Crab Rangoon Dip With Wonton Chips

Servings: 6   Cooking Time: 18 Minutes

Ingredients:

- Wonton Chips:
- 1 (12-ounce) package wonton wrappers
- vegetable oil
- sea salt
- Crab Rangoon Dip:
- 8 ounces cream cheese, softened
- ¾ cup sour cream
- 1 teaspoon Worcestershire sauce
- 1½ teaspoons soy sauce
- 1 teaspoon sesame oil
- ⅛ teaspoon ground cayenne pepper
- ¼ teaspoon salt
- freshly ground black pepper
- 8 ounces cooked crabmeat
- 1 cup grated white Cheddar cheese
- ⅓ cup chopped scallions
- paprika (for garnish)

Directions:

1. Cut the wonton wrappers in half diagonally to form triangles. Working in batches, lay the wonton triangles on a flat surface and brush or spray both sides with vegetable oil.

2. Preheat the toaster oven to 370°F.

3. Place about 10 to 12 wonton triangles in the air fryer oven, letting them overlap slightly. Air-fry for just 2 minutes. Transfer the wonton chips to a large bowl and season immediately with sea salt. (You'll hear the chips start to spin around in the air fryer oven when they are almost done.) Repeat with the rest of wontons (keeping those fishing hands at bay!).

4. To make the dip, combine the cream cheese, sour cream, Worcestershire sauce, soy sauce, sesame oil, cayenne pepper, salt, and freshly ground black pepper in a bowl. Mix well and then fold in the crabmeat, Cheddar cheese, and scallions.

5. Transfer the dip to a 7-inch ceramic baking pan or shallow casserole dish. Sprinkle paprika on top and cover the dish with aluminum foil. Lower the dish into the air fryer oven using a sling made of aluminum foil (fold a piece of aluminum foil into a strip about 2-inches wide by 24-inches long). Air-fry for 11 minutes. Remove the aluminum foil and air-fry for another 5 minutes to finish cooking and brown the top. Serve hot with the wonton chips.

Garden Fresh Bruschetta

Servings: 6

Cooking Time: 5 Minutes

Ingredients:

- 1/2 cup Parmigiano-Reggiano cheese
- 2 cloves garlic (or to taste)
- 2 tablespoons balsamic vinegar
- 1/3 cup pine nuts
- 1 loaf crusty Italian bread
- 1 or 2 fresh tomatoes, sliced or chopped
- Salt and pepper to taste
- 4 cups fresh basil leaves, stems removed

Directions:

1. With shredding disk inserted, shred cheese in food processor. Remove from food processor and set aside.

2. Insert S-blade in food processor and coarsely chop basil leaves and garlic. Add vinegar and pulse a few times. Add pine nuts to basil mixture and pulse until coarsely chopped. With food processor running, drizzle olive oil through feed chute until ingredients are coated and spreadable. Add half of the already grated Parmesan cheese and pulse until just blended.

3. To assemble: Slice crusty bread on diagonal, place on toaster oven size cookie sheet. On each piece of bread, spread basil mixture. Place tomatoes on top of basil, add salt and pepper to taste. Sprinkle some of the remaining cheese on top.

4. Place in preheated 350°F toaster oven for 5 minutes or until cheese melts and bread is warmed. Serve as an appetizer.

Rosemary-roasted Potatoes

Servings:4

Cooking Time: 40 Minutes

Ingredients:

- 1 pound russet potatoes, or baby potatoes, cut into 1-inch chunks
- 2 tablespoons olive oil
- 1 teaspoon garlic powder
- 1 teaspoon dried rosemary
- Sea salt, for seasoning
- Freshly ground black pepper, for seasoning

Directions:

1. Preheat the toaster oven on AIR FRY to 400°F for 5 minutes.

2. In a large bowl, toss the potatoes with the oil, garlic powder, and rosemary. Season with salt and pepper.

3. Place the air-fryer basket in the baking tray and spread the potatoes in a single layer in the basket. You may have to do two batches. Cover the first batch loosely with foil to keep it warm while you cook the second batch.

4. In position 2, AIR FRY on 400°F for 20 minutes, shaking the basket at 10 minutes, until the potatoes are tender and golden brown. Repeat with the remaining potatoes and serve.

BEEF PORK AND LAMB

Spicy Flank Steak With Fresh Tomato-corn Salsa

Servings: 4

Cooking Time: 20 Minutes

Ingredients:

- 2 large tomatoes, chopped
- 1 cup fresh (or canned) corn
- ½ English cucumber, chopped
- ¼ red onion, chopped
- 1 tablespoon jalapeño pepper, chopped
- 1 tablespoon fresh cilantro, chopped
- Sea salt, for seasoning
- Freshly ground black pepper, for seasoning
- 1 pound extra-lean beef flank steak, trimmed of fat
- Olive oil, for brushing
- 1 teaspoon garlic powder
- 1 teaspoon chili powder

Directions:

1. Preheat the toaster oven to 450°F on BROIL for 5 minutes.
2. In a small bowl, stir the tomato, corn, cucumber, onion, jalapeño, and cilantro, and season with salt and pepper.
3. Rub the steak all over with the oil and then season with garlic powder, chili powder, salt, and pepper.
4. Place the air-fryer basket in the baking tray and arrange the steak in the basket.
5. In position 2, broil for 20 minutes, turning halfway through, until browned and with an internal temperature of 140°F, for medium-rare.
6. Let the steak rest for 10 minutes and then cut it very thinly against the grain.
7. Serve with the salsa.

Crunchy Fried Pork Loin Chops

Servings: 3

Cooking Time: 12 Minutes

Ingredients:

- 1 cup All-purpose flour or tapioca flour
- 1 Large egg(s), well beaten
- 1½ cups Seasoned Italian-style dried bread crumbs (gluten-free, if a concern)
- 3 4- to 5-ounce boneless center-cut pork loin chops
- Vegetable oil spray

Directions:

1. Preheat the toaster oven to 350°F .

2. Set up and fill three shallow soup plates or small pie plates on your counter: one for the flour, one for the beaten egg(s), and one for the bread crumbs.

3. Dredge a pork chop in the flour, coating both sides as well as around the edge. Gently shake off any excess, then dip the chop in the egg(s), again coating both sides and the edge. Let any excess egg slip back into the rest, then set the chop in the bread crumbs, turning it and pressing gently to coat well on both sides and the edge. Coat the pork chop all over with vegetable oil spray and set aside so you can dredge, coat, and spray the additional chop(s).

4. Set the chops in the air fryer oven with as much air space between them as possible. Air-fry undisturbed for 12 minutes, or until brown and crunchy and an instant-read meat thermometer inserted into the center of a chop registers 145°F.

5. Use kitchen tongs to transfer the chops to a wire rack. Cool for 5 minutes before serving.

Barbeque Ribs

Servings: 4

Cooking Time: 35 Minutes

Ingredients:

- 2 pounds pork spareribs or baby back ribs, silver skin removed
- 2 tablespoons brown sugar
- 1 teaspoon chili powder
- 1 teaspoon dry mustard
- Sea salt, for seasoning
- Freshly ground black pepper, for seasoning
- Oil spray (hand-pumped)
- 1 cup barbeque sauce

Directions:

1. Preheat the toaster oven to 375°F on AIR FRY for 5 minutes.
2. Cut the ribs into 4 bone sections or to fit in the basket.
3. In a small bowl, combine the brown sugar, chili powder, and mustard, and rub it all over the ribs.
4. Season the ribs with salt and pepper.
5. Place the air-fryer basket in the baking tray and spray it generously with the oil.
6. Arrange the ribs in the basket. There can be overlap if necessary.
7. In position 2, air fry for 35 minutes, turning halfway through, until the ribs are tender, browned, and crisp.
8. Baste the ribs with the barbeque sauce and serve.

Chicken Fried Steak

Servings: 4

Cooking Time: 15 Minutes

Ingredients:

- 2 eggs
- ½ cup buttermilk
- 1½ cups flour
- ¾ teaspoon salt
- ½ teaspoon pepper
- 1 pound beef cube steaks
- salt and pepper
- oil for misting or cooking spray

Directions:

1. Beat together eggs and buttermilk in a shallow dish.
2. In another shallow dish, stir together the flour, ½ teaspoon salt, and ¼ teaspoon pepper.
3. Season cube steaks with remaining salt and pepper to taste. Dip in flour, buttermilk egg wash, and then flour again.
4. Spray both sides of steaks with oil or cooking spray.
5. Cooking in 2 batches, place steaks in air fryer oven in single layer. Air-fry at 360°F for 10 minutes. Spray tops of steaks with oil and cook 5 minutes or until meat is well done.
6. Repeat to cook remaining steaks.

Beef Vegetable Stew

Servings: 4

Cooking Time: 120 Minutes

Ingredients:

- 1 pound lean stewing beef, cut into 1-inch chunks
- 2 carrots, diced
- 2 celery stalks
- 1 large potato, diced
- ½ sweet onion, chopped
- 2 teaspoons minced garlic
- 1 (15-ounce) can diced tomatoes, with juices
- 1 teaspoon sea salt
- ½ teaspoon freshly ground black pepper
- 1 cup low-sodium beef broth
- 3 tablespoons all-purpose flour
- 1 cup frozen peas

Directions:

1. Place the rack in position 1 and preheat the toaster oven to 375°F on BAKE for 5 minutes.

2. In a 1½-quart casserole dish, combine the beef, carrots, celery, potato, onion, garlic, tomatoes, salt, and pepper.

3. In a small bowl, stir the broth and flour until well combined. Add the broth mixture to the beef mixture and stir to combine.

4. Cover with foil or a lid and bake for 2 hours, stirring each time you reset the timer, until the meat is very tender.

5. Stir in the peas and let stand for 10 minutes. Serve.

Sweet Potato–crusted Pork Rib Chops

Servings: 2

Cooking Time: 14 Minutes

Ingredients:

- 2 Large egg white(s), well beaten
- 1½ cups (about 6 ounces) Crushed sweet potato chips (certified gluten-free, if a concern)
- 1 teaspoon Ground cinnamon
- 1 teaspoon Ground dried ginger
- 1 teaspoon Table salt (optional)
- 2 10-ounce, 1-inch-thick bone-in pork rib chop(s)

Directions:

1. Preheat the toaster oven to 375°F .

2. Set up and fill two shallow soup plates or small pie plates on your counter: one for the beaten egg white(s); and one for the crushed chips, mixed with the cinnamon, ginger, and salt (if using).

3. Dip a chop in the egg white(s), coating it on both sides as well as the edges. Let the excess egg white slip back into the rest, then set it in the crushed chip mixture. Turn it several times, pressing gently, until evenly coated on both sides and the edges. If necessary, set the chop aside and coat the remaining chop(s).

4. Set the chop(s) in the air fryer oven with as much air space between them as possible. Air-fry undisturbed for 12 minutes, or until crunchy and browned and an instant-read meat thermometer inserted into the center of a chop (without touching bone) registers 145°F. If the machine is at 360°F, you may need to add 2 minutes to the cooking time.

5. Use kitchen tongs to transfer the chop(s) to a wire rack. Cool for 2 or 3 minutes before serving.

Indian Fry Bread Tacos

Ingredients:

- 1 cup all-purpose flour
- 1½ teaspoons salt, divided
- 1½ teaspoons baking powder
- ¼ cup milk
- ¼ cup warm water
- ½ pound lean ground beef
- One 14.5-ounce can pinto beans, drained and rinsed
- 1 tablespoon taco seasoning
- ½ cup shredded cheddar cheese
- 2 cups shredded lettuce
- ¼ cup black olives, chopped
- 1 Roma tomato, diced
- 1 avocado, diced
- 1 lime

Directions:

1. In a large bowl, whisk together the flour, 1 teaspoon of the salt, and baking powder. Make a well in the center and add in the milk and water. Form a ball and gently knead the dough four times. Cover the bowl with a damp towel, and set aside.

2. Preheat the toaster oven to 380°F.

3. In a medium bowl, mix together the ground beef, beans, and taco seasoning. Crumble the meat mixture into the air fryer oven and air-fry for 5 minutes; toss the meat and cook an additional 2 to 3 minutes, or until cooked fully. Place the cooked meat in a bowl for taco assembly; season with the remaining ½ teaspoon salt as desired.

4. On a floured surface, place the dough. Cut the dough into 4 equal parts. Using a rolling pin, roll out each piece of dough to 5 inches in diameter. Spray the dough with cooking spray and place in the air fryer oven, working in batches as needed. Air-fry for 3 minutes, flip over, spray with cooking spray, and air-fry for an additional 1 to 3 minutes, until golden and puffy.

5. To assemble, place the fry breads on a serving platter. Equally divide the meat and bean mixture on top of the fry bread. Divide the cheese, lettuce, olives, tomatoes, and avocado among the four tacos. Squeeze lime over the top prior to serving.

Pork Loin

Servings: 8

Cooking Time: 50 Minutes

Ingredients:

- 1 tablespoon lime juice
- 1 tablespoon orange marmalade
- 1 teaspoon coarse brown mustard
- 1 teaspoon curry powder
- 1 teaspoon dried lemongrass
- 2-pound boneless pork loin roast
- salt and pepper
- cooking spray

Directions:

1. Mix together the lime juice, marmalade, mustard, curry powder, and lemongrass.
2. Rub mixture all over the surface of the pork loin. Season to taste with salt and pepper.
3. Spray air fryer oven with nonstick spray and place pork roast diagonally in the pan.
4. Air-fry at 360°F for approximately 50 minutes, until roast registers 130°F on a meat thermometer.
5. Wrap roast in foil and let rest for 10minutes before slicing.

Herbed Lamb Burgers

Servings: 4

Cooking Time: 15 Minutes

Ingredients:

- 1 pound lean ground lamb
- 1 large egg
- 1 tablespoon fresh parsley, chopped
- 2 teaspoons fresh mint, chopped
- 1 teaspoon minced garlic
- ¼ teaspoon sea salt
- ⅛ teaspoon freshly ground black pepper
- Olive oil spray (hand-pumped)
- 4 whole-wheat buns
- ¼ cup store-bought tzatziki sauce
- 1 tomato, cut into slices
- 4 thin red onion slices
- ½ cup shredded lettuce

Directions:

1. Preheat the toaster oven to 350°F on CONVECTION BROIL for 5 minutes.
2. In a large bowl, mix the lamb, egg, parsley, mint, garlic, salt, and pepper. Form the mixture into 4 patties.
3. Place the air-fryer basket in the baking tray and place the burger patties in the basket. Lightly spray the patties with the oil on both sides.
4. In position 2, broil for 15 minutes, turning halfway through.
5. Serve on the buns topped with tzatziki sauce, tomato, onion, and lettuce.

Beef, Onion, And Pepper Shish Kebab

Servings: 4

Cooking Time: 20 Minutes

Ingredients:

- Marinade:
- 2 tablespoons olive oil
- ½ cup dry red wine
- 1 tablespoon soy sauce
- 1 teaspoon chili powder
- 1 teaspoon Worcestershire sauce
- 1 teaspoon garlic powder
- 1 teaspoon spicy brown mustard
- 1 teaspoon brown sugar
- 8 onion quarters, approximately 2 × 2-inch pieces
- 8 bell pepper quarters, 2 × 2-inch pieces
- 1 pound lean boneless beef (sirloin, round steak, London broil), cut into 8 2-inch cubes
- 4 8-inch metal or wooden (bamboo) skewers

Directions:

1. Combine the marinade ingredients in a large bowl. Add the onion, peppers, and beef. Refrigerate, covered, for at least 1 hour or

2. Skewer alternating beef, pepper, and onion pieces. Brush with the marinade mixture and place the skewers on a broiling rack with the pan underneath.

3. BROIL for 5 minutes, remove the pan with the skewers from the oven, turn the skewers, brush again, then broil for another 5 minutes. Repeat turning and brushing every 5 minutes, until the peppers and onions are well cooked and browned to your preference.

Vietnamese Beef Lettuce Wraps

Servings: 4   Cooking Time: 12 Minutes

Ingredients:

- ⅓ cup low-sodium soy sauce
- 2 teaspoons fish sauce
- 2 teaspoons brown sugar
- 1 tablespoon chili paste
- juice of 1 lime
- 2 cloves garlic, minced
- 2 teaspoons fresh ginger, minced
- 1 pound beef sirloin
- Sauce
- ⅓ cup low-sodium soy sauce
- juice of 2 limes
- 1 tablespoon mirin wine
- 2 teaspoons chili paste
- Serving
- 1 head butter lettuce
- ½ cup julienned carrots
- ½ cup julienned cucumber
- ½ cup sliced radishes, sliced into half moons
- 2 cups cooked rice noodles
- ⅓ cup chopped peanuts

Directions:

1. Combine the soy sauce, fish sauce, brown sugar, chili paste, lime juice, garlic and ginger in a bowl. Slice the beef into thin slices, then cut those slices in half. Add the beef to the marinade and marinate for 1 to 3 hours in the refrigerator. When you are ready to cook, remove the steak from the refrigerator and let it sit at room temperature for 30 minutes.

2. Preheat the toaster oven to 400°F.

3. Transfer the beef and marinade to the air fryer oven. Air-fry at 400°F for 12 minutes.

4. While the beef is cooking, prepare a wrap-building station. Combine the soy sauce, lime juice, mirin wine and chili paste in a bowl and transfer to a little pouring vessel. Separate the lettuce leaves from the head of lettuce and put them in a serving bowl. Place the carrots, cucumber, radish, rice noodles and chopped peanuts all in separate serving bowls.

5. When the beef has finished cooking, transfer it to another serving bowl and invite your guests to build their wraps. To build the wraps, place some beef in a lettuce leaf and top with carrots, cucumbers, some rice noodles and chopped peanuts. Drizzle a little sauce over top, fold the lettuce around the ingredients and enjoy!

Barbecue-style London Broil

Servings: 5

Cooking Time: 17 Minutes

Ingredients:

- ¾ teaspoon Mild smoked paprika
- ¾ teaspoon Dried oregano
- ¾ teaspoon Table salt
- ¾ teaspoon Ground black pepper
- ¼ teaspoon Garlic powder
- ¼ teaspoon Onion powder
- 1½ pounds Beef London broil (in one piece)
- Olive oil spray

Directions:

1. Preheat the toaster oven to 400°F.

2. Mix the smoked paprika, oregano, salt, pepper, garlic powder, and onion powder in a small bowl until uniform.

3. Pat and rub this mixture across all surfaces of the beef. Lightly coat the beef on all sides with olive oil spray.

4. When the machine is at temperature, lay the London broil flat in the air fryer oven and air-fry undisturbed for 8 minutes for the small batch, 10 minutes for the medium batch, or 12 minutes for the large batch for medium-rare, until an instant-read meat thermometer inserted into the center of the meat registers 130°F (not USDA-approved). Add 1, 2, or 3 minutes, respectively (based on the size of the cut) for medium, until an instant-read meat thermometer registers 135°F (not USDA-approved). Or add 3, 4, or 5 minutes respectively for medium, until an instant-read meat thermometer registers 145°F (USDA-approved).

5. Use kitchen tongs to transfer the London broil to a cutting board. Let the meat rest for 10 minutes. It needs a long time for the juices to be reincorporated into the meat's fibers. Carve it against the grain into very thin (less than ¼-inch-thick) slices to serve.

Lime-ginger Pork Tenderloin

Servings: 4

Cooking Time: 26 Minutes

Ingredients:

- ½ cup packed dark brown sugar
- Juice of ½ lime
- 2 teaspoons fresh ginger, peeled and grated
- 1 teaspoon minced garlic
- 2 (1-pound) extra-lean pork tenderloins, trimmed of fat
- Sea salt, for seasoning
- Freshly ground black pepper, for seasoning
- 1 tablespoon olive oil

Directions:

1. Preheat the toaster oven to 400°F on CONVECTION BAKE for 5 minutes.
2. In a small bowl, stir the sugar, lime juice, ginger, and garlic together.
3. Lightly season the pork tenderloins all over with salt and pepper.
4. Heat the oil in a large skillet over medium-high heat. Brown the pork on all sides, about 6 minutes in total.
5. Place the air-fryer basket in the baking tray and place the tenderloins in the basket.
6. Brush the pork all over with the ginger-lime mixture.
7. In position 2, bake for 20 minutes, basting the pork at 10 minutes, until it reaches an internal temperature of about 145°F.
8. Let the pork rest for 10 minutes and serve.

Pork Cutlets With Almond-lemon Crust

Servings: 3

Cooking Time: 14 Minutes

Ingredients:

- ¾ cup Almond flour
- ¾ cup Plain dried bread crumbs (gluten-free, if a concern)
- 1½ teaspoons Finely grated lemon zest
- 1¼ teaspoons Table salt
- ¾ teaspoon Garlic powder
- ¾ teaspoon Dried oregano
- 1 Large egg white(s)
- 2 tablespoons Water
- 3 6-ounce center-cut boneless pork loin chops (about ¾ inch thick)
- Olive oil spray

Directions:

1. Preheat the toaster oven to 375°F .

2. Mix the almond flour, bread crumbs, lemon zest, salt, garlic powder, and dried oregano in a large bowl until well combined.

3. Whisk the egg white(s) and water in a shallow soup plate or small pie plate until uniform.

4. Dip a chop in the egg white mixture, turning it to coat all sides, even the ends. Let any excess egg white mixture slip back into the rest, then set it in the almond flour mixture. Turn it several times, pressing gently to coat it evenly. Generously coat the chop with olive oil spray, then set aside to dip and coat the remaining chop(s).

5. Set the chops in the air fryer oven with as much air space between them as possible. Air-fry undisturbed for 12 minutes, or until browned and crunchy. You may need to add 2 minutes to the cooking time if the machine is at 360°F.

6. Use kitchen tongs to transfer the chops to a wire rack. Cool for a few minutes before serving.

VEGETABLES AND VEGETARIAN

Sweet Potato Puffs

Servings: 18   Cooking Time: 35 Minutes

Ingredients:

- 3 8- to 10-ounce sweet potatoes
- 1 cup Seasoned Italian-style dried bread crumbs
- 3 tablespoons All-purpose flour
- 3 tablespoons Instant mashed potato flakes
- ¾ teaspoon Onion powder
- ¾ teaspoon Table salt
- Olive oil spray

Directions:

1. Preheat the toaster oven to 350°F .

2. Prick the sweet potatoes in four or five different places with the tines of a flatware fork (not in a line but all around the sweet potatoes).

3. When the machine is at temperature, set the sweet potatoes in the air fryer oven with as much air space between them as possible. Air-fry undisturbed for 20 minutes.

4. Use kitchen tongs to transfer the sweet potatoes to a wire rack. (They will still be firm; they are only partially cooked.) Cool for 10 to 15 minutes. Meanwhile, increase the machine's temperature to 400°F. Spread the bread crumbs on a dinner plate.

5. Peel the sweet potatoes. Shred them through the large holes of a box grater into a large bowl. Stir in the flour, potato flakes, onion powder, and salt until well combined.

6. Scoop up 2 tablespoons of the sweet potato mixture. Form it into a small puff, a cylinder about like a Tater Tot. Set this cylinder in the bread crumbs. Gently roll it around to coat on all sides, even the ends. Set aside on a cutting board and continue making more puffs: 11 more for a small batch, 17 more for a medium batch, or 23 more for a large batch.

7. Generously coat the puffs with olive oil spray on all sides. Set the puffs in the air fryer oven with as much air space between them as possible. They should not be touching, but even a fraction of an inch will work well. Air-fry undisturbed for 15 minutes, or until lightly browned and crunchy.

8. Gently turn the contents of the air fryer oven out onto a wire rack. Cool the puffs for a couple of minutes before serving.

Ranch Potatoes

Servings: 2

Cooking Time: 50 Minutes

Ingredients:

- ➢ 2 medium russet potatoes, scrubbed and cut lengthwise into ¼-inch strips
- ➢ 1 medium onion, chopped
- ➢ 2 tablespoons vegetable oil
- ➢ 2 tablespoons barbecue sauce
- ➢ ¼ teaspoon hot sauce
- ➢ Salt and freshly ground black pepper

Directions:

1. Preheat the toaster oven to 400° F.
2. Combine all the ingredients in a medium bowl, mixing well and adjusting the seasonings to taste.
3. Place equal portions of the potatoes on two 12 × 12-inch squares of heavy-duty aluminum foil. Fold up the edges of the foil to form a sealed packet and place on the oven rack.
4. BAKE for 40 minutes, or until the potatoes are tender. Carefully open the packet and fold back the foil.
5. BROIL 10 minutes, or until the potatoes are browned.

Fried Green Tomatoes With Sriracha Mayo

Servings: 4   Cooking Time: 12 Minutes

Ingredients:

- 3 green tomatoes
- salt and freshly ground black pepper
- ⅓ cup all-purpose flour
- 2 eggs
- ½ cup buttermilk
- 1 cup panko breadcrumbs
- 1 cup cornmeal
- olive oil, in a spray bottle
- fresh thyme sprigs or chopped fresh chives
- Sriracha Mayo
- ½ cup mayonnaise
- 1 to 2 tablespoons sriracha hot sauce
- 1 tablespoon milk

Directions:

1. Cut the tomatoes in ¼-inch slices. Pat them dry with a clean kitchen towel and season generously with salt and pepper.

2. Set up a dredging station using three shallow dishes. Place the flour in the first shallow dish, whisk the eggs and buttermilk together in the second dish, and combine the panko breadcrumbs and cornmeal in the third dish.

3. Preheat the toaster oven to 400°F.

4. Dredge the tomato slices in flour to coat on all sides. Then dip them into the egg mixture and finally press them into the breadcrumbs to coat all sides of the tomato.

5. Spray or brush the air-fryer oven with olive oil. Transfer 3 to 4 tomato slices into the air fryer oven and spray the top with olive oil. Air-fry the tomatoes at 400°F for 8 minutes. Flip them over, spray the other side with oil and air-fry for an additional 4 minutes until golden brown.

6. While the tomatoes are cooking, make the sriracha mayo. Combine the mayonnaise, 1 tablespoon of the sriracha hot sauce and milk in a small bowl. Stir well until the mixture is smooth. Add more sriracha sauce to taste.

7. When the tomatoes are done, transfer them to a cooling rack or a platter lined with paper towels so the bottom does not get soggy. Before serving, carefully stack the all the tomatoes into air fryer oven and air-fry at 350°F for 1 to 2 minutes to heat them back up.

8. Serve the fried green tomatoes hot with the sriracha mayo on the side. Season one last time with salt and freshly ground black pepper and garnish with sprigs of fresh thyme or chopped fresh chives.

Brussels Sprout And Ham Salad

Servings: 3

Cooking Time: 12 Minutes

Ingredients:

- ➤ 1 pound 2-inch-in-length Brussels sprouts, quartered through the stem
- ➤ 6 ounces Smoked ham steak, any rind removed, diced (gluten-free, if a concern)
- ➤ ¼ teaspoon Caraway seeds
- ➤ Vegetable oil spray
- ➤ ¼ cup Brine from a jar of pickles (gluten-free, if a concern)
- ➤ ¾ teaspoon Ground black pepper

Directions:

1. Preheat the toaster oven to 375°F .

2. Toss the Brussels sprout quarters, ham, and caraway seeds in a bowl until well combined. Generously coat the top of the mixture with vegetable oil spray, toss again, spray again, and repeat a couple of times until the vegetables and ham are glistening.

3. When the machine is at temperature, scrape the contents of the bowl into the air fryer oven, spreading it into as close to one layer as you can. Air-fry for 12 minutes, tossing and rearranging the pieces at least twice so that any covered or touching parts are eventually exposed to the air currents, until the Brussels sprouts are tender and a little brown at the edges.

4. Dump the contents of the air fryer oven into a serving bowl. Scrape any caraway seeds from the bottom of the air fryer oven or the tray under the pan attachment into the bowl as well. Add the pickle brine and pepper. Toss well to coat. Serve warm.

Wilted Brussels Sprout Slaw

Servings: 4

Cooking Time: 18 Minutes

Ingredients:

- 2 Thick-cut bacon strip(s), halved widthwise (gluten-free, if a concern)
- 4½ cups (about 1 pound 2 ounces) Bagged shredded Brussels sprouts
- ¼ teaspoon Table salt
- 2 tablespoons White balsamic vinegar
- 2 teaspoons Worcestershire sauce (gluten-free, if a concern)
- 1 teaspoon Dijon mustard (gluten-free, if a concern)
- ¼ teaspoon Ground black pepper

Directions:

1. Preheat the toaster oven to 375°F .

2. When the machine is at temperature, lay the bacon strip halves in the air fryer oven in one layer and air-fry for 10 minutes, or until crisp.

3. Use kitchen tongs to transfer the bacon pieces to a wire rack. Put the shredded Brussels sprouts in a large bowl. Drain any fat from the pan or the tray under the pan onto the Brussels sprouts. Add the salt and toss well to coat.

4. Put the Brussels sprout shreds in the air fryer oven, spreading them out into as close to an even layer as you can. Air-fry for 8 minutes, tossing the air fryer oven's contents at least three times, until wilted and lightly browned.

5. Pour the contents of the air fryer oven into a serving bowl. Chop the bacon and add it to the Brussels sprouts. Add the vinegar, Worcestershire sauce, mustard, and pepper. Toss well to blend the dressing and coat the Brussels sprout shreds. Serve warm.

Eggplant And Tomato Slices

Servings: 4

Cooking Time: 36 Minutes

Ingredients:

- 2 tablespoons olive oil
- ¼ teaspoon garlic powder
- 4½-inch-thick slices eggplant
- 4 ¼-inch-thick slices fresh tomato
- 2 tablespoons tomato sauce or salsa
- ½ cup shredded Parmesan cheese
- Salt and freshly ground black pepper to taste
- 2 tablespoons chopped fresh basil, cilantro, parsley, or oregano

Directions:

1. Whisk together the oil and garlic powder in a small bowl. Brush each eggplant slice with the mixture and place in an oiled or nonstick 8½ × 8½ × 2-inch square baking (cake) pan.

2. BROIL for 20 minutes. Remove the pan from the oven and turn the pieces with tongs. Top each with a slice of tomato and broil another 10 minutes, or until tender. Remove the pan from the oven, brush each slice with tomato sauce or salsa, and sprinkle generously with Parmesan cheese. Season to taste with salt and pepper. Broil again for 6 minutes, until the tops are browned.

3. Garnish with the fresh herb and serve.

Asparagus Fries

Servings: 4

Cooking Time: 5 Minutes

Ingredients:

- 12 ounces fresh asparagus spears with tough ends trimmed off
- 2 egg whites
- ¼ cup water
- ¾ cup panko breadcrumbs
- ¼ cup grated Parmesan cheese, plus 2 tablespoons
- ¼ teaspoon salt
- oil for misting or cooking spray

Directions:

1. Preheat the toaster oven to 390°F.
2. In a shallow dish, beat egg whites and water until slightly foamy.
3. In another shallow dish, combine panko, Parmesan, and salt.
4. Dip asparagus spears in egg, then roll in crumbs. Spray with oil or cooking spray.
5. Place a layer of asparagus in air fryer oven, leaving just a little space in between each spear. Stack another layer on top, crosswise. Air-fry at 390°F for 5 minutes, until crispy and golden brown.
6. Repeat to cook remaining asparagus.

Blistered Green Beans

Servings: 3

Cooking Time: 10 Minutes

Ingredients:

- ¾ pound Green beans, trimmed on both ends
- 1½ tablespoons Olive oil
- 3 tablespoons Pine nuts
- 1½ tablespoons Balsamic vinegar
- 1½ teaspoons Minced garlic
- ¾ teaspoon Table salt
- ¾ teaspoon Ground black pepper

Directions:

1. Preheat the toaster oven to 400°F.

2. Toss the green beans and oil in a large bowl until all the green beans are glistening.

3. When the machine is at temperature, pile the green beans into the air fryer oven. Air-fry for 10 minutes, tossing often to rearrange the green beans in the air fryer oven, or until blistered and tender.

4. Dump the contents of the air fryer oven into a serving bowl. Add the pine nuts, vinegar, garlic, salt, and pepper. Toss well to coat and combine. Serve warm or at room temperature.

Salmon Salad With Steamboat Dressing

Servings: 4

Cooking Time: 18 Minutes

Ingredients:

- ¼ teaspoon salt
- 1½ teaspoons dried dill weed
- 1 tablespoon fresh lemon juice
- 8 ounces fresh or frozen salmon fillet (skin on)
- 8 cups shredded romaine, Boston, or other leaf lettuce
- 8 spears cooked asparagus, cut in 1-inch pieces
- 8 cherry tomatoes, halved or quartered

Directions:

1. Mix the salt and dill weed together. Rub the lemon juice over the salmon on both sides and sprinkle the dill and salt all over. Refrigerate for 15 to 20 minutes.

2. Make Steamboat Dressing and refrigerate while cooking salmon and preparing salad.

3. Cook salmon in air fryer oven at 330°F for 18 minutes. Cooking time will vary depending on thickness of fillets. When done, salmon should flake with fork but still be moist and tender.

4. Remove salmon from air fryer oven and cool slightly. At this point, the skin should slide off easily. Cut salmon into 4 pieces and discard skin.

5. Divide the lettuce among 4 plates. Scatter asparagus spears and tomato pieces evenly over the lettuce, allowing roughly 2 whole spears and 2 whole cherry tomatoes per plate.

6. Top each salad with one portion of the salmon and drizzle with a tablespoon of dressing. Serve with additional dressing to pass at the table.

Potato Skins

Servings: 4

Cooking Time: 20 Minutes

Ingredients:

- 4 potato shells

Directions:

1. Place 4 potato shells in an oiled or nonstick 8½ × 8½ × 2-inch square baking (cake) pan.

2. Brush, sprinkle, and fill with a variety of seasonings or ingredients.

3. BROIL 20 minutes, or until browned and crisped to your preference.

Street Corn

Servings: 4

Cooking Time: 10 Minutes

Ingredients:

- ➢ 1 tablespoon butter
- ➢ 4 ears corn
- ➢ ⅓ cup plain Greek yogurt
- ➢ 2 tablespoons Parmesan cheese
- ➢ ½ teaspoon paprika
- ➢ ½ teaspoon garlic powder
- ➢ ¼ teaspoon salt
- ➢ ¼ teaspoon black pepper
- ➢ ¼ cup finely chopped cilantro

Directions:

1. Preheat the toaster oven to 400°F.

2. In a medium microwave-safe bowl, melt the butter in the microwave. Lightly brush the outside of the ears of corn with the melted butter.

3. Place the corn into the air fryer oven and air-fry for 5 minutes, flip the corn, and cook another 5 minutes.

4. Meanwhile, in a medium bowl, mix the yogurt, cheese, paprika, garlic powder, salt, and pepper. Set aside.

5. Carefully remove the corn from the air fryer oven and let cool 3 minutes. Brush the outside edges with the yogurt mixture and top with fresh chopped cilantro. Serve immediately.

Roasted Garlic

Servings: 1

Cooking Time: 20 Minutes

Ingredients:

➢   3 whole garlic buds

➢   3 tablespoons olive oil

➢   Salt and freshly ground black pepper

Directions:

1.   Preheat the toaster oven to 450° F.

2.   Place the garlic buds in an oiled or nonstick 8½ × 8½ × 2-inch square baking (cake) pan.

3.   BAKE, uncovered, for 20 minutes, or until the buds are tender when pierced with a skewer or sharp knife. When cool enough to handle, peel and mash the baked cloves with a fork into the olive oil. Season with salt and pepper to taste.

Rolled Chinese (napa) Cabbage With Chickpea Filling

Servings: 4

Cooking Time: 46 Minutes

Ingredients:

- ➢ 6 Chinese cabbage leaves, approximately 7 inches long
- ➢ Filling:
- ➢ 2 tablespoons low-fat ricotta cheese or Yogurt Cheese Spread
- ➢ 1 cup canned chickpeas (garbanzos), drained and mashed
- ➢ 1 teaspoon lemon juice
- ➢ Salt and butcher's pepper to taste
- ➢ 2 tablespoons olive oil for brushing
- ➢ 2 tablespoons chopped almonds

Directions:

1. Layer an 8½ × 8½ × 2-inch square baking (cake) pan with the cabbage leaves and add enough water to barely cover them.

2. BROIL 5 minutes, turn the leaves with tongs, and broil another 5 minutes, or until the leaves are partially cooked and just pliable. Spread the leaves on paper towels to drain and cool.

3. Mix the filling ingredients together in a medium bowl and adjust the seasonings to taste. Place equal portions of filling 2 inches from the stem end (base of the leaf) and roll up the leaf, enclosing the filling. Place each roll with the leaf edge down in an oiled or 8½ × 8½ × 2-inch square baking (cake) pan. Sprinkle with the almonds. Cover the pan with aluminum foil.

4. BAKE at 400° F. for 30 minutes, or until the rolls are tender. Remove the cover.

5. BROIL 6 minutes, or until the almonds and cabbage leaves are lightly browned.

Simply Sweet Potatoes

Servings: 2

Cooking Time: 35 Minutes

Ingredients:

- ➤ 2 medium sweet potatoes, scrubbed and slit on top
- ➤ ¼ teaspoon ground thyme per potato
- ➤ 1 tablespoon lemon juice per potato
- ➤ ½ teaspoon margarine per potato
- ➤ Salt and freshly ground black pepper

Directions:

1. Preheat the toaster oven to 425° F.

2. BAKE the potatoes on the oven rack for 35 minutes, or until tender.

3. Open the slit and fluff the sweet potato pulp with a fork. Sprinkle the pulp with equal portions of thyme, lemon juice, and margarine. Fluff again. Season with salt and pepper to taste.

DESSERTS

Fried Oreos

Servings: 12

Cooking Time: 7 Minutes

Ingredients:

- ➢ 1 Large egg white(s)
- ➢ 2 tablespoons Water
- ➢ 1 cup Graham cracker crumbs
- ➢ 12 Original-size Oreos (not minis or king-size)
- ➢ Vegetable oil spray

Directions:

1. Preheat the toaster oven to 375°F .

2. Set up and fill two shallow soup plates or small pie plates on your counter: one for the egg white(s), whisked with the water until foamy; and one for the graham cracker crumbs.

3. Dip a cookie in the egg white mixture, turning several times to coat well. Let any excess egg white mixture slip back into the rest, then set the cookie in the crumbs. Turn several times to coat evenly, pressing gently. You want an even but not thick crust. However, make sure that the cookie is fully coated and that the filling is sealed inside. Lightly coat the cookie on all sides with vegetable oil spray. Set aside and continue dipping and coating the remaining cookies.

4. Set the coated cookies in the oven with as much air space between them as possible. Air-fry undisturbed for 6 minutes, or until the coating is golden brown and set. If the machine is at 360°F, the cookies may need 1 minute more to cook and set.

5. Use a nonstick-safe spatula to transfer the cookies to a wire rack. Cool for at least 5 minutes before serving.

Chocolate Caramel Pecan Cupcakes

Servings: 6

Cooking Time: 20 Minutes

Ingredients:

- 6 tablespoons all-purpose flour
- 6 tablespoons unsweetened cocoa powder
- ¼ teaspoon baking soda
- ¼ teaspoon baking powder
- ⅛ teaspoon table salt
- 6 tablespoons unsalted butter, softened
- ½ cup granulated sugar
- 1 large egg
- ½ teaspoon pure vanilla extract
- ½ cup sour cream
- BUTTERCREAM FROSTING
- ¼ cup unsalted butter, softened
- 1 ¾ cups confectioners' sugar
- 2 to 3 tablespoons half-and-half or milk
- 1 teaspoon pure vanilla extract
- Caramel ice cream topping
- ¼ cup caramelized chopped pecans

Directions:

1. Preheat the toaster oven to 350°F. Line a 6-cup muffin pan with cupcake papers.

2. Whisk the flour, cocoa, baking soda, baking powder, and salt in a small bowl; set aside.

3. Beat the butter and granulated sugar in a large bowl with a handheld mixer at medium-high speed for 2 minutes, or until the mixture is light and creamy. Beat in the egg well. Beat in the vanilla.

4. On low speed, beat in the flour mixture in thirds, alternating with the sour cream, beginning and ending with the flour mixture. The batter will be thick.

5. Spoon the batter evenly into the prepared cupcake cups, filling each about three-quarters full. Bake for 18 to 20 minutes, or until a wooden pick inserted into the center comes out clean. Place on a wire rack and let cool completely.

6. Meanwhile, make the frosting: Beat the butter in a large bowl using a handheld mixer on medium-high speed until creamy. Gradually beat in the confectioners' sugar. Beat in 2 tablespoons of half-and-half and the vanilla. Beat in the remaining tablespoon of half-and-half, as needed, until the frosting is of desired consistency.

7. Frost each cooled cupcake. Drizzle the caramel topping in thin, decorative stripes over the frosting. Top with the caramelized pecans.

Fried Snickers Bars

Servings: 8

Cooking Time: 4 Minutes

Ingredients:

- ⅓ cup All-purpose flour
- 1 Large egg white(s), beaten until foamy
- 1½ cups (6 ounces) Vanilla wafer cookie crumbs
- 8 Fun-size (0.6-ounce/17-gram) Snickers bars, frozen
- Vegetable oil spray

Directions:

1. Preheat the toaster oven to 400°F.

2. Set up and fill three shallow soup plates or small pie plates on your counter: one for the flour, one for the beaten egg white(s), and one for the cookie crumbs.

3. Unwrap the frozen candy bars. Dip one in the flour, turning it to coat on all sides. Gently stir any excess, then set it in the beaten egg white(s). Turn it to coat all sides, even the ends, then let any excess egg white slip back into the rest. Set the candy bar in the cookie crumbs. Turn to coat on all sides, even the ends. Dip the candy bar back in the egg white(s) a second time, then into the cookie crumbs a second time, making sure you have an even coating all around. Coat the covered candy bar all over with vegetable oil spray. Set aside so you can dip and coat the remaining candy bars.

4. Set the coated candy bars in the pan with as much air space between them as possible. Air-fry undisturbed for 4 minutes, or until golden brown.

5. Remove the pan from the machine and let the candy bars cool in the pan for 10 minutes. Use a nonstick-safe spatula to transfer them to a wire rack and cool for 5 minutes more before chowing down.

Triple Chocolate Brownies

Servings: 16

Cooking Time: 25 Minutes

Ingredients:

- ⅓ cup salted butter, room temperature, plus extra for greasing the baking dish
- ¾ cup brown sugar
- 2 large eggs
- 1 teaspoon vanilla extract
- ½ cup all-purpose flour
- ¼ cup cocoa powder
- ¼ teaspoon baking powder
- ⅛ teaspoon salt
- ½ cup dark chocolate chips
- ¼ cup white chocolate chips

Directions:

1. Place the rack in position 1 and preheat the oven to 325°F on BAKE for 5 minutes.
2. Lightly grease a 6-inch-square baking dish with butter.
3. In a large bowl, beat together the butter and sugar with an electric hand beater or a whisk until combined. Add the eggs and vanilla and beat to combine.
4. Beat in the flour, cocoa powder, baking powder, and salt until just combined.
5. Stir in dark chocolate and white chocolate chips, then spoon the batter into the prepared dish.
6. Bake for 25 minutes or until a knife inserted in the center comes out mostly clean.
7. Cool in the baking dish and serve.

Soft Peanut Butter Cookies

Servings: 12

Cooking Time: 20 Minutes

Ingredients:

- ➢ 1/2 cup vegetable shortening
- ➢ 1/2 cup peanut butter
- ➢ 1 1/4 cups light brown sugar
- ➢ 1 egg
- ➢ 1 teaspoon vanilla
- ➢ 1/2 teaspoon salt
- ➢ 1 1/2 cups flour
- ➢ 1 teaspoon baking soda
- ➢ Sugar crystals

Directions:

1. Preheat the toaster oven to 275°F.

2. Using the flat beater attachment, beat shortening, peanut butter, brown sugar, egg, and vanilla at a medium setting until well blended.

3. Reduce speed to low and gradually add dry ingredients until blended. Dough will be crumbly.

4. Roll 3 tablespoon-size portions of the dough into a ball. Place on ungreased cookie sheet.

5. Press to 1/2-inch thick. Sprinkle with sugar crystals.

6. Bake 18 to 20 minutes. Do not overcook.

Not Key Lime, Lime Pie

Servings: 3   Cooking Time: 27 Minutes

Ingredients:

- 1 tablespoon grated lime zest
- 3 large egg yolks
- 1 (14-ounce) can sweetened condensed milk
- ½ cup fresh lime juice
- 1 ¾ cups graham cracker crumbs (about 12 full graham crackers)
- ⅓ cup granulated sugar
- ⅛ teaspoon table salt
- ½ cup unsalted butter, melted
- Nonstick cooking spray
- WHIPPED CREAM
- 1 cup heavy cream
- ⅓ cup confectioners' sugar

Directions:

1. Preheat the toaster oven to 350°F.

2. Whisk the lime zest and egg yolks in a large bowl for 1 minute. Whisk in the sweetened condensed milk and lime juice. Set aside to thicken while you prepare the crust.

3. Stir the graham cracker crumbs, granulated sugar, and salt in a medium bowl. Pour the butter over the mixture and mix until combined and moist. Press the crust evenly into the bottom and up the sides of a 9-inch pie plate. Pack tightly using the back of a large spoon. Bake for 10 minutes. Let cool on a cooling rack.

4. When the crust is completely cool, pour the lime filling inside. Bake for 15 to 17 minutes, or until the center is set (it will still jiggle a bit). Allow the pie to cool completely at room temperature. Spray plastic wrap with nonstick cooking spray and place on the pie. Refrigerate for at least 3 hours or overnight.

5. Beat the cream in a large bowl with an electric mixer at medium-high speed until soft peaks form. Add the confectioners' sugar, one tablespoon at a time, and continue to beat until stiff peaks form. Dollop, pipe, or spread the whipped cream over the pie before serving. Refrigerate leftovers for up to 3 days.

Make-ahead Oatmeal-raisin Cookies

Servings: 8

Cooking Time: 45 Minutes

Ingredients:

- 1 cup (5 ounces) all-purpose flour
- ¾ teaspoon table salt
- ½ teaspoon baking soda
- ¼ teaspoon ground cinnamon
- ¾ cup (5¼ ounces) dark brown sugar
- ½ cup (3½ ounces) granulated sugar
- ½ cup vegetable oil
- 4 tablespoons unsalted butter, melted and cooled
- 1 large egg plus 1 large yolk
- 1 teaspoon vanilla extract
- 3 cups (9 ounces) old-fashioned rolled oats
- ½ cup raisins

Directions:

1. Adjust toaster oven rack to middle position and preheat the toaster oven to 350 degrees. Line large and small rimmed baking sheets with parchment paper. Whisk flour, salt, baking soda, and cinnamon together in bowl.

2. Whisk brown sugar and granulated sugar together in medium bowl. Whisk in oil and melted butter until combined. Whisk in egg and yolk and vanilla until smooth. Gently stir in flour mixture with rubber spatula until soft dough forms. Fold in oats and raisins until evenly distributed (mixture will be stiff).

3. Working with 3 tablespoons dough at a time, roll into balls. Space desired number of dough balls at least 1½ inches apart on prepared small sheet; space remaining dough balls evenly on prepared large sheet. Using bottom of greased dry measuring cup, press each ball until 2½ inches in diameter.

4. Bake small sheet of cookies until edges are just beginning to brown and centers are still soft but not wet, 10 to 15 minutes. Let cookies cool slightly on sheet. Serve warm or at room temperature.

5. Freeze remaining large sheet of cookies until firm, about 1 hour. Transfer cookies to 1-gallon zipper-lock bag and freeze for up to 1 month. Bake frozen cookies as directed; do not thaw.

Mini Gingerbread Bundt Cakes

Servings: 16

Cooking Time: 24 Minutes

Ingredients:

- 3 cups all-purpose flour
- 1/4 cup baking cocoa
- 1 tablespoon baking soda
- 1 teaspoon ground cinnamon
- 1 teaspoon ground ginger
- 1 teaspoon salt
- 1/4 teaspoon ground cloves
- 1/4 teaspoon ground nutmeg
- 1 cup butter, softened
- 1 1/4 cups milk

- 1 cup packed dark brown sugar
- 1 cup molasses
- 2 large eggs
- 1 cup mini chocolate chips Glaze: 1 package (12 oz.) semi-sweet chocolate chips
- 1/3 cup heavy cream
- 2 tablespoons butter
- 2 tablespoons light corn syrup
- Chopped crystallized ginger

Directions:

1. Preheat the toaster oven to 350°F. Spray mini bundt pans with nonstick cooking spray. Dust with flour.

2. In a medium bowl, stir together flour, cocoa, baking soda, cinnamon, ginger, salt, cloves and nutmeg.

3. In a large mixer bowl, beat butter until creamy. Gradually beat in milk, brown sugar, molasses and eggs until well blended.

4. Reduce speed to LOW. Slowly add flour mixture until blended. Stir in chocolate chips.

5. Pour into prepared bundt pans.

6. Bake 20 to 24 minutes or until toothpick inserted in center comes out clean.

7. Cool on wire rack 10 minutes. Invert onto cooling rack and cool completely.

8. In a microwavable bowl, stir together 1 cup chocolate chips, heavy cream, butter and corn syrup.

9. Microwave on MEDIUM power 1 minute or until chips are shiny. Stir until mixture is smooth.

10. Spread glaze over top of each mini bundt and sprinkle with crystallized ginger.

Cowboy Cookies

Servings: 3

Cooking Time: 14 Minutes

Ingredients:

- Recommended Hamilton Beach® Product: Stand Mixers
- 1 cup butter
- 1 cup sugar
- 1 cup light brown sugar
- 2 eggs
- 2 cups flour
- 1 teaspoon baking soda
- ½ teaspoon baking powder
- ½ teaspoon salt
- 2 cups oatmeal
- 1 tablespoon vanilla
- 12 ounces chocolate chips
- 1 ½ cups coconut

Directions:

1. Preheat the toaster oven to 350°F.

2. With flat beater attachment, cream together butter, sugar, and brown sugar at a medium setting until well blended. Mix in vanilla and eggs. Reduce speed and gradually add flour, baking soda, baking powder, and salt mix until smooth.

3. On a low setting, mix in oatmeal, chocolate chips, and coconut until well mixed. Drop rounded spoon full onto ungreased cookie sheet.

4. Bake on middle rack of oven for 12 to 14 minutes.

Make-ahead Chocolate Chip Cookies

Servings: 12

Cooking Time: 45 Minutes

Ingredients:

- 2⅛ cups (10⅔ ounces) all-purpose flour
- ½ teaspoon baking soda
- ½ teaspoon table salt
- 1 cup packed (7 ounces) light brown sugar
- ½ cup (3½ ounces)granulated sugar
- 12 tablespoons unsalted butter, melted and cooled
- 1 large egg plus 1 large yolk
- 2 teaspoons vanilla extract
- 1 cup (6 ounces) semisweet chocolate chips

Directions:

1. Adjust toaster oven rack to middle position and preheat the toaster oven to 350 degrees. Line large and small rimmed baking sheets with parchment paper. Whisk flour, baking soda, and salt together in bowl.

2. Whisk brown sugar and granulated sugar together in medium bowl. Whisk in melted butter until combined. Whisk in egg and yolk and vanilla until smooth. Gently stir in flour mixture with rubber spatula until soft dough forms. Fold in chocolate chips.

3. Working with 2 tablespoons dough at a time, roll into balls. Space desired number of dough balls at least 1½ inches apart on prepared small sheet; space remaining dough balls evenly on prepared large sheet. Using bottom of greased dry measuring cup, press each ball until 2 inches in diameter.

4. Bake small sheet of cookies until edges are just beginning to brown and centers are soft and puffy, 10 to 15 minutes. Let cookies cool slightly on sheet. Serve warm or at room temperature.

5. Freeze remaining large sheet of cookies until firm, about 1 hour. Transfer cookies to 1-gallon zipper-lock bag and freeze for up to 1 month. Bake frozen cookies as directed; do not thaw.

Apple Strudel

Servings: 2   Cooking Time: 90 Minutes

Ingredients:

- 2 Golden Delicious apples (14 ounces), peeled, cored, and cut into ½-inch pieces
- 1½ tablespoons granulated sugar
- ¼ teaspoon grated lemon zest plus 1 teaspoon juice
- ⅛ teaspoon ground cinnamon
- ⅛ teaspoon ground ginger
- ⅛ teaspoon table salt, divided
- 2 tablespoons golden raisins
- 1 tablespoon panko bread crumbs
- 3½ tablespoons unsalted butter, melted
- 1½ teaspoons confectioners' sugar, plus extra for serving
- 7 (14 by 9-inch) phyllo sheets, thawed

Directions:

1. Toss apples, granulated sugar, lemon zest and juice, cinnamon, ginger, and pinch salt together in large bowl. Cover and microwave until apples are softened, 2 to 4 minutes, stirring once halfway through microwaving. Let apples sit, covered, for 5 minutes. Transfer apples to colander set in second large bowl and let drain, reserving liquid. Return apples to bowl; stir in raisins and panko.

2. Adjust toaster oven rack to middle position and preheat the toaster oven to 350 degrees. Spray small rimmed baking sheet with vegetable oil spray. Stir remaining pinch salt into melted butter.

3. Place 16½ by 12-inch sheet of parchment paper on counter with long side parallel to edge of counter. Place 1 phyllo sheet on parchment with long side parallel to edge of counter. Place confectioners' sugar in fine-mesh strainer. Lightly brush sheet with melted butter and dust sparingly with confectioners' sugar. Repeat with remaining 6 phyllo sheets, melted butter, and confectioners' sugar, stacking sheets one on top of other as you go.

4. Arrange apple mixture in 2½ by 10-inch rectangle 2 inches from bottom of phyllo and about 2 inches from each side. Using parchment, fold sides of phyllo over filling, then fold bottom edge of phyllo over filling. Brush folded portions of phyllo with reserved apple liquid. Fold top edge over filling, making sure top and bottom edges overlap by about 1 inch. (If they do not overlap, unfold, rearrange filling into slightly narrower strip, and refold.) Press firmly to seal. Using thin metal spatula, transfer strudel to prepared sheet. Lightly brush top and sides of strudel with remaining apple liquid.

5. Bake until golden brown, 25 to 30 minutes, rotating sheet halfway through baking. Using thin metal spatula, immediately transfer strudel to cutting board. Let cool for 3 minutes. Slice strudel and let cool for at least 20 minutes. Serve warm or at room temperature, dusting with extra confectioners' sugar before serving.

Blueberry Cheesecake Tartlets

Servings: 9

Cooking Time: 6 Minutes

Ingredients:

- 8 ounces cream cheese, softened
- ¼ cup sugar
- 1 egg
- ½ teaspoon vanilla extract
- zest of 2 lemons, divided
- 9 mini graham cracker tartlet shells
- 2 cups blueberries
- ½ teaspoon ground cinnamon
- juice of ½ lemon
- ¼ cup apricot preserves

Directions:

1. Preheat the toaster oven to 330°F.

2. Combine the cream cheese, sugar, egg, vanilla and the zest of one lemon in a medium bowl and blend until smooth by hand or with an electric hand mixer. Pour the cream cheese mixture into the tartlet shells.

3. Air-fry 3 tartlets at a time at 330°F for 6 minutes, rotating them in the air fryer oven halfway through the cooking time.

4. Combine the blueberries, cinnamon, zest of one lemon and juice of half a lemon in a bowl. Melt the apricot preserves in the microwave or over low heat in a saucepan. Pour the apricot preserves over the blueberries and gently toss to coat.

5. Allow the cheesecakes to cool completely and then top each one with some of the blueberry mixture. Garnish the tartlets with a little sugared lemon peel and refrigerate until you are ready to serve.

CPSIA information can be obtained
at www.ICGtesting.com
Printed in the USA
LVHW020223230323
742377LV00003B/49